C000002193

Translator: Gina Schofield

This edition first published in 1993 by
Sunburst Books, Deacon House, 65 Old Church Street,
London, SW3 5BS

Copyright © Editorial LIBSA, Narciso Serra, 25 - Tel 433 54 07 -
28007 MADRID
4.ª EDICION 1991
Copyright English language text © 1993 Sunburst Books

All rights reserved. No part of this publication may be reproduced,
stored in a retrieval system, or transmitted in any form or by any
means, electronic, mechanical, photocopying, recording, or otherwise,
without the prior written permission of the Publisher.

ISBN 1 85778 008 6

Printed and bound in China

FRENCH
COOKING

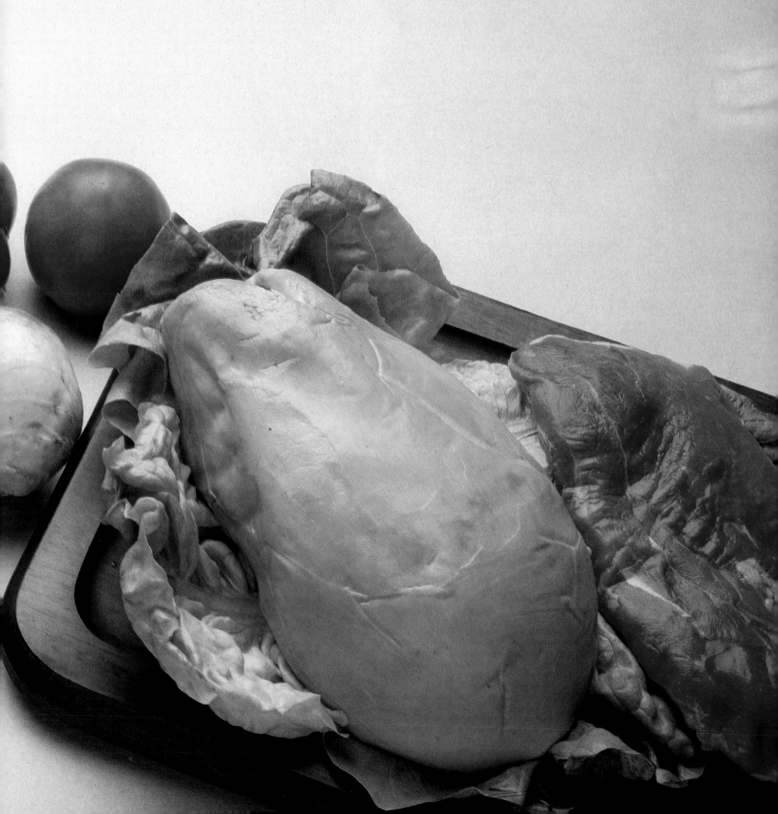

CONTENTS

INTRODUCTION

French cuisine is, with some justification, famous across the world and is thought by many - especially the French themselves - to be the best in the world. This may or may not be true, but it certainly includes some of the most imaginative and delicious dishes ever invented.

When we think of French cooking we tend to think first of haute cuisine, that is, cooking as an art practised by a few exceptional chefs employed by the royal, the rich and the famous. The great chefs, restaurateurs and gourmets of France have left a rich legacy of recipes created in the restaurants and palaces of Europe. Famous, almost legendary, names include Antonin Carême, Brillat-Savarin, Joseph Favre, Dugléré and, of course, the partnership of César Ritz and Auguste Escoffier. The finest and, often, the most extravagant ingredients are combined to create rich sauces and a subtle, inimitable blending of flavours. Some of the great classics of haute cuisine are included in the following pages - Beef Stroganoff, Chicken Henri IV, Crème Agnès Sorel, Crêpes Suzette, Omelette Charles Monselet, Oysters François Villon and Tournedos Curnonsky. These delicious and wickedly indulgent recipes are still the perfect choice for a luxurious dinner party when you want to impress and thoroughly spoil special guests.

For more modest, everyday needs we must turn to French provincial or bourgeois cooking. The high quality of the ingredients is no less important and the housewife from Provence is no less fussy about the ripeness of the vegetables, the freshness of the fish and the proper cut of meat than the chef from Paris. Like all country cooking, French provincial cuisine is based around readily available ingredients, but, given that France extends from the chilly Channel shores of Brittany and Normandy to the sun-baked beaches of the Mediterranean, any collection of such recipes offers immense scope. Unlike haute cuisine, provincial cooking employs every last scrap and tends to make full use of cheaper, although no less delicious, cuts of meat. The sauces are less rich - you won't see many truffles, for example - but the dishes have a succulence all their own. Some of the regional specialities you will find in the following pages include Artichokes Country-Style, Auvergne Stuffed Cabbage, Mushrooms Gascony, Navarin Printanier, Breton Pigs' Trotters and Normandy Pork Chops.

Bon apetit!

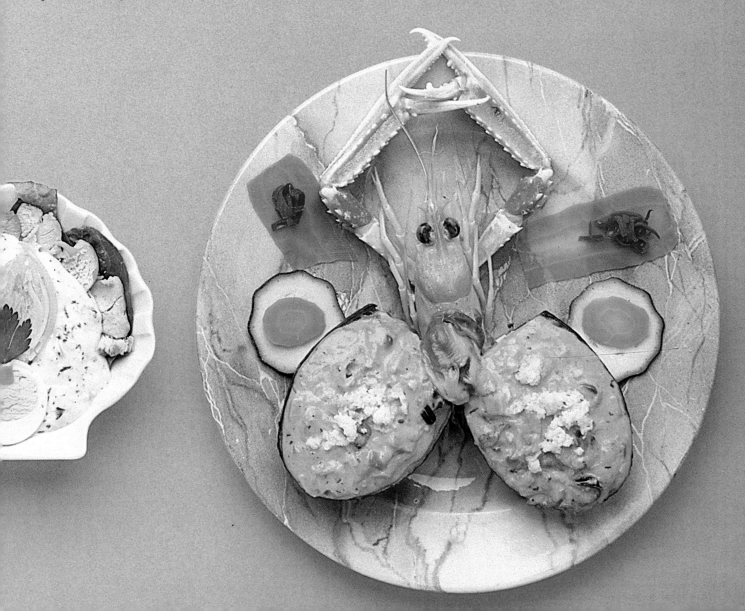

STOCKS, ROUX AND SAUCES

Stocks are broths, juices or fats that are used to make sauces, stews or roasts. A roux is one of the elements in a stock. The ways that they differ are described below.

White stock: this is a colourless stock prepared with white meat, bones and green vegetables or herbs. It is used as the basis for white sauces or white meat stews, as well as for poaching poultry.

Red meat stock: this is made with beef or veal, bones, green vegetables or herbs and fat, lard or oil. It is used as the basis for red meat sauces for grilled meat and red meat stews.

Fish stock: this is made with fish bones, fish trimmings and equal quantities of white wine and water. It is flavoured with chopped onions, parsley, thyme, bay leaves, lemon juice and mushrooms and is used for sauces for fish dishes – sauce Normande and white wine sauce, for example – and also for coating fish before grilling or poaching.

Vegetable stock: this is used in vegetarian cooking and is made with chopped green vegetables, carrots, celery and onions, sautéed in vegetable oil and diluted with water. It is flavoured with parsley, thyme and bay leaves.

Stock for making gelée: this is made with 2 kg/4½ lb veal hock, 1.5 kg/3¼ lb bones, cut in half, and 1.5 kg/3¼ lb calves' feet. These must all be lightly roasted in the oven.

To gel the mixture, add 3 calf's feet, boned and blanched and 250 g/9 oz blanched strips of bacon rind. For flavouring, add 20 g/⅔ oz carrots, 200g/7 oz onions, 60 g/2 oz leeks, 60 g/2oz celery and a large bouquet garni. Add 8.5 litres/14 ½ pints of water and cook for 6 hours.

Fumet: this is made with fish bones, fish heads, several slices of onion and shallot, some sprigs of parsley, a sprig of thyme and a little butter. Leave them to sweat for 15 minutes over very low heat and add 500 ml/18 fl oz water, a pinch of salt and, ideally, sliced mushrooms.

Bring to the boil over a high heat and simmer for 10-15 minutes. Then strain and store in a non-metallic dish. Reduce to the necessary amount when needed or use for coating fish prior to cooking and keep as a base for making the sauce.

Roux are thickeners for sauces. There are three types of roux:

White roux: this is made with 120 g/ 4 oz butter and 150 g/5 oz flour, cooked together for 5 minutes over low heat, stirring constantly with a spatula.

Golden roux: this is made by mixing 120 g/4 oz butter with 150 g/5 oz flour. Melt the butter and add the flour, then cook at a low temperature in the oven, for a long period, stirring frequently so that the mixture takes on a medium brown colour, but without allowing the fat or flour to burn.

To obtain a perfect mix which will make a smooth sauce without lumps, it is advisable to mix a cold roux with a hot base, or a hot roux with a cold base.

Beurre manié: for 600 ml/1 pint stock, place 60 g/2 oz butter in a bowl and cream with 30 g/1 oz flour using a fork. Then mix in the stock, adding a little at a time and stirring thoroughly. Do not add the next piece until the last one has been fully incorporated.

BÉARNAISE SAUCE

2 shallots, peeled and finely chopped
1 tbsp chopped tarragon
100 ml/3½ fl oz tarragon vinegar
3 egg yolks
150 g/5 oz butter, melted
salt
freshly ground black pepper

Put the shallots, tarragon and vinegar in a pan and bring to the boil. Remove from the heat and set aside to cool.

Place the vinegar mixture in a heatproof bowl over a pan of hot, but not boiling water. Add the egg yolks and 2 tsp of cold water. Beat over low heat until smooth and thickened. Gradually stir in the butter. Season with salt and pepper and strain through muslin.

BÉCHAMEL SAUCE

60 g/2 oz butter
60 g/2 oz flour
330 ml/11 fl oz hot milk
salt
freshly ground black pepper

Melt the butter in a saucepan over low heat. Add the flour and cook, stirring constantly, for 2-3 minutes.

Once the mixture resembles a golden liquid paste, remove the pan from the heat and add all the hot milk at once, stirring well to remove any lumps.

Return the pan to moderate heat and cook, stirring constantly, until the mixture thickens. Season with salt and pepper.

BORDELAISE SAUCE

1 bottle red Burgundy wine
2 tsp chopped shallots, cooked
300 ml/10 fl oz strong beef stock
60 g/2 oz butter
150 g/5 oz beef marrow, poached and drained
1 tbsp chopped parsley (optional)

Place the wine in a flameproof casserole with the shallots, bring to the boil and reduce to 100 ml/3½ fl oz. Add the stock and cook for at least 30 minutes. Strain and add the butter and marrow.

If desired, add the chopped parsley.

HOLLANDAISE SAUCE

4 egg yolks
1 tbsp hot water
250 g/9 oz butter
salt
freshly ground black pepper
juice of 1 lemon

Beat together the egg yolks in a small heatproof bowl. Beat in the water. Set the bowl over a pan of hot, but not boiling water and gradually add the butter, little by little, stirring constantly. Do not allow the mixture to boil. Season with salt and pepper and add lemon juice to taste.

Serve immediately or keep warm in a *bain marie* or over a pan of hot water until required. Do not allow the sauce to overheat or it will curdle.

SAUCE IVOIRE

60 g/2 oz butter
1 tbsp flour
450 ml/16 fl oz chicken stock
salt
freshly ground black pepper
100 ml/3½ fl oz single cream
3 tbsp jellied chicken stock

First make a *sauce suprême*. Melt the butter

in a pan over moderate heat and stir in the flour. Stir in the stock and continue cooking, stirring constantly, until the mixture thickens.

Season with salt and pepper and add the cream. Bring the sauce to the boil and remove the pan from the heat. This completes the *sauce suprême*.

To make a *sauce ivoire*, add the jellied chicken stock.

GRIVICHE SAUCE

3 hard-boiled eggs, shelled and halved
1 tbsp chopped mixed herbs
1 tsp French mustard

225 ml/8 fl oz olive oil
1 tsp white wine vinegar
salt
freshly ground black pepper

Remove the yolks from the eggs and mash in a small bowl, together with the herbs and the mustard, until creamy. Gradually beat in the oil, drop by drop, until completely incorporated. Stir in the vinegar and season with salt and pepper. Finely chop the egg whites and stir them into the sauce.

MORNAY SAUCE

500 ml/18 fl oz Béchamel sauce
100 g/3¹/₂ oz Gruyère cheese, grated
salt
freshly ground black pepper

First make the Béchamel sauce, following the recipe given on page 6, but using 500 ml/18 fl oz milk and increasing the quantities of the other ingredients proportionately.

When the sauce is hot, stir in the grated cheese and season with salt and pepper to taste.

NANTUA SAUCE

500 ml/18 fl oz Béchamel sauce
200 ml/7 fl oz single cream
100 g/3¹/₂ oz crab paste
1 tsp butter

Stir together the Béchamel sauce and the single cream over low heat until reduced. Strain through clean muslin. Stir in the crab paste and the butter. Keep warm until serving.

DUXELLES

30 g/1 oz butter
1 tbsp oil
30 g/1 oz onion, chopped
30 g/1 oz shallots, chopped
250 g/9 oz mushroom stalks, finely chopped
1 tsp chopped parsley
salt
freshly ground black pepper

Heat the butter with the oil in a frying-pan and sauté the onions and shallots for 5-8 minutes. Add the mushroom stalks, pressing them down to extract their juices. Sauté and then add the parsley and the seasoning to taste.

Lucullus Duck Pâté (see page 8)

STARTERS

HERRING FILLETS WITH TOMATO

Serves 8

sea salt
16 herring fillets
1 sugar cube
2 tsp vinegar
freshly ground black pepper
500 g/1 lb 2 oz ripe tomatoes, skinned, seeded and chopped

Garnish:
1 lemon, thinly sliced

Lightly scatter a layer of sea salt in a dish and place the fish fillets on top. Scatter over more sea salt and set aside for 6 hours.

Rinse the fish to remove excess salt and place them in a flameproof dish. Preheat the grill to hot.

Put the sugar, vinegar and pepper in a saucepan and heat until the sugar begins to turn golden brown. Add the tomatoes and bring to the boil. Pour the sauce over the herring fillets and place under the hot grill for a few seconds.

Serve cold garnished with lemon slices.

LUCULLUS DUCK PÂTÉ

Serves 6-8

1 x 1.5 kg/3¹/₂ lb duck with giblets
1 kg/2¹/₄ lb pork loin
salt
freshly ground black pepper
¹/₄ tsp mixed spice
2 eggs
100 g/3¹/₂ oz bottled truffles, thinly sliced and juice reserved
60 ml /2 fl oz brandy
150 g/5 oz liver pâté
250 g/9 oz streaky bacon, rinds removed and thinly sliced

Garnish (optional)
truffle slices

Cut along the length of the duck's back and remove the carcass without breaking the skin. Then remove all the adjoining flesh. Reserve the skin and the duck liver from the giblets.

To prepare the pork loin, cut off the fat.

Mince the pork and the duck meat finely together. Work in a food processor or mash the mince in a mortar with salt, pepper and the mixed spice. Stir in the eggs, truffle juice and brandy. Work this mixture together, gradually incorporating the liver pâté at the same time.

Preheat oven to 180° C/350° F, gas mark 4.

Lay out the duck skin in preparation for the filling. Slice the reserved duck liver. Place the filling along the length of the centre of the skin, together with the liver and truffles. Sew up the skin with trussing thread so that the duck resembles a thick sausage. Cover with the bacon slices and wrap in foil. Tie the package together with string and bake in the oven for 1¹/₂ hours.

Remove the duck from the oven, unwrap the package and set aside to cool. Serve sliced and garnished with slices of truffle, if liked.

AVOCADO PEARS WITH SEAFOOD

Serves 4

4 avocado pears
75 g/2¹/₂ oz lobster meat, chopped
75 g/2¹/₂ oz peeled prawns, chopped
75 g/2¹/₂ oz mushrooms, chopped
salt
freshly ground black pepper
4 tsp lemon juice
4 tsp olive oil
300 ml/10 fl oz mayonnaise
2 tsp grated radish
¹/₂ tsp French mustard
2 tsp tomato ketchup
2 tsp dry sherry
4 tsp whipped cream
1 hard-boiled egg, shelled and chopped
4 oysters (optional)

Cut the avocado pears in half lengthways, remove the stones and scoop out the flesh. Reserve the avocado shells.

Mix together the lobster meat, prawns, mushrooms and avocado flesh in a glass dish. Season with salt and pepper, pour over the lemon juice and oil and chill in the refrigerator for at least 1 hour.

Meanwhile, mix together the mayonnaise, radish, mustard, ketchup, sherry and cream. Stir into the avocado

mixture and use to fill the reserved avocado shells. Sprinkle over the chopped hard-boiled egg.

Arrange the filled avocado halves on a serving dish and garnish with oysters in their shells, if liked. Serve chilled.

CHICKEN SHELLS WITH MAYONNAISE

Serves 6

1 lettuce
500 g/1 lb 2 oz cooked chicken, sliced
200 ml/7 fl oz mayonnaise
2 hard-boiled eggs, shelled and sliced

This dish is traditionally served in empty scallop shells, although china or silver shells would be equally suitable.

Line the bottom of each shell with a lettuce leaf and place the chicken slices on top. Cover with the mayonnaise and garnish each shell with a slice of hard-boiled egg and some lettuce heart.

ROQUEFORT CHEESE BALLS

Serves 8

250 g/9 oz Roquefort cheese, crumbled
2 tsp finely chopped celery
2 tsp chopped chives
2 tsp paprika

Rub the Roquefort cheese through a wire strainer.

Mix the celery and chives into the cheese until the mixture is thoroughly blended. Shape the mixture into balls a little smaller than a walnut and sprinkle with the paprika before serving.

Top: Chicken Shells with Mayonnaise
Bottom: Avocado Pears with Seafood

CHAMPIGNONS À LA FAVORITE

Serves 8

60 g/2 oz butter
16 large cap mushrooms, stalks removed
salt
freshly ground black pepper
100 ml/3½ fl oz veal stock
300 ml/10 fl oz Madeira
150 g/5 oz cooked tongue, chopped
8 small pieces bread, fried in butter

Preheat the oven to 200° C/400° F, gas mark 6. Grease a large ovenproof dish with half the butter. Arrange the mushroom caps in a single layer in the prepared dish. Season with salt and pepper and dot with with the remaining butter. Cook in the oven for 7 minutes.

Meanwhile, bring the stock and the Madeira to the boil and continue cooking until reduced. Stir in the tongue.

Arrange the fried bread on a serving plate, top with the mushrooms, garnish with the sauce and serve immediately.

Champagne-style Pâté

CHAMPAGNE-STYLE PÂTÉ

Serves 12

750 g/1 lb 10 oz foie-gras or chicken liver
  pâté, finely chopped
250 g/9 oz minced pork
250 g/9 oz pork fat, finely chopped
¼ tsp ground cloves
¼ tsp grated nutmeg
salt
freshly ground black pepper
1 bay leaf

Preheat the oven to 180° C/350° F, gas mark 4.

Mix together the foie-gras or pâté, minced pork, pork fat, spices and seasoning until thoroughly combined. Turn the mixture into a terrine, top with the bay leaf and cook in the oven for 45 minutes.

Remove the terrine from oven and set aside to cool. Turn out the pâté, cut into slices and serve cold.

LOBSTER COCKTAIL

Serves 4

600 g/l lb 5 oz cooked lobster meat
4 tomatoes, skinned, seeded and finely chopped
150 ml/5 fl oz mayonnaise
4 lettuce leaves
4 cooked mushroom caps
100 ml/3½ fl oz brandy
1 tsp tomato ketchup

Cut some of the lobster into 8 slices and dice the remainder. Mix together the diced lobster and tomatoes. Stir in the mayonnaise.

Line the bottom of 4 wide champagne glasses with a lettuce leaf each and fill with the lobster mixture. Garnish each glass with 2 slices of lobster and a mushroom cap.

Combine the brandy and ketchup and sprinkle over the cocktails. Serve chilled.

SOUPS

ONION SOUP

Serves 8

100 g/3¹/₂ oz butter
2 large onions, peeled and finely sliced
3 litres/5¹/₄ pints consommé (clear soup)
salt
freshly ground black pepper
16 small slices French bread
150 g/5 oz Gruyère cheese, grated

Preheat the oven to 220° C/425° F, gas mark 7.

Melt the butter in a frying-pan and fry the onions for 8-10 minutes until golden. Add the consommé, season with salt and pepper and bring to the boil.

Meanwhile, place alternate layers of bread and grated cheese in a soup tureen or 8 individual soup bowls. Pour over the onion broth, cover with a final layer of cheese and brown briefly in the oven.

LES HALLES ONION SOUP

Serves 8

60 g/2 oz butter
250 g/9 oz onions, peeled and slice
30 g/1 oz flour
2 litres/3¹/₂ pints clear stock
salt •
freshly ground black pepper
60 g/2 oz croûtons
200 g/7 oz cheese, grated

Melt the butter and fry the onions for 8-10 minutes until golden. Stir in the flour and cook for 1-2 minutes until lightly coloured. Remove the pan from the heat and gradually stir in the stock. Return to the heat and cook for about 20 minutes.

Preheat the oven to 220° C/425° F, gas mark 7.

Season the soup and strain into a soup tureen (this is optional). Sprinkle with the croûtons and grated cheese and brown briefly in the oven. Alternatively, serve the cheese separately.

Note: Les Halles was a famous market in Paris, dating from the Middle Ages and still in use until the 1970s. This filling soup may have evolved as a traditional morning snack for the hard-working porters.

EGG CONSOMMÉ

Serves 8

12 egg yolks
3 tbsp brandy
salt
freshly ground black pepper
3 litres/5¹/₄ pints cold meat stock
100 g/3¹/₂ oz bread slices, toasted

Beat together the egg yolks, brandy and seasoning in a saucepan. Place over low heat and gradually add the meat stock, stirring constantly. Bring the mixture to the boil, stirring constantly. Place the toasted bread slices in the bottom of a soup tureen and pour over the boiling soup.

Top: Onion Soup
Bottom: Egg Consommé

CRÈME AGNÈS SOREL

Serves 8

150 g/5 oz butter
100 g/3½ oz flour
1 litre/1¾ pints chicken stock
1 small chicken, cooked, skinned, boned and
   chopped
300 ml/10 fl oz single cream
800 g/1¾ lb mushrooms, chopped
300 ml/10 fl oz Béchamel sauce
100 g/3½ oz cooked tongue, cut into strips
salt
freshly ground black pepper

Melt half the butter in a saucepan and
gradually mix in the flour, stirring
constantly. Remove the pan from the heat
and gradually stir in the stock. Return the
pan to the heat and bring to the boil,
stirring constantly.

Reserve the chopped chicken breast and
mince the remaining meat. Mix the
minced chicken with half the remaining
butter and half the cream. Pour the
mixture into the stock and cook over low
heat.

Remove the pan from the heat, and stir
in half the remaining butter and all the
remaining cream. Return to low heat for
15 minutes, stirring frequently.

Meanwhile, melt the remaining butter
and sauté the mushrooms for 4-5 minutes,
season and stir into the soup. Add the
Béchamel sauce and heat through for 2
minutes. Stir in the reserved chopped
chicken breast meat and the tongue,
season, heat through again and serve
immediately.

Note: Agnès Sorel was a celebrated cook
and the mistress of King Charles VII. Her
name is always used for this garnish.

CRAYFISH BISQUE

Serves 8

24 prepared crayfish
200 g/7 oz butter
100 g/3½ oz mirepoix★
200 ml/7 fl oz white wine
200 ml/7 fl oz fish stock
60 ml/2 fl oz brandy
salt
freshly ground black pepper
2.3 litres/4 pints consommé
225 g/8 oz rice
100 ml/3½ fl oz single cream
1 bouquet garni

Melt half the butter and sauté the
mirepoix over low heat until softened.
Increase the heat to high, add the crayfish
and sauté until the shells take on a bright
red colour. Add the white wine, fish stock
and half the brandy. Season with salt and

pepper. Cover and cook for 10-12 minutes, depending on the size of the crayfish.

Meanwhile, bring the consommé to the boil and cook the rice. Drain and reserve the cooking liquid.

Peel the crayfish, keeping the tails and a dozen shells to one side. Combine the remaining peeled crayfish with the rice and most of its cooking liquid, together with the mirepoix and liquid from the pan. Purée in a blender or food processor and place in a saucepan. If necessary, add more of the cooking liquid to obtain the consistency for a creamed soup. Heat to boiling point.

To serve, stir in the cream, remaining brandy and butter. Garnish the soup with the reserved crayfish shells and tails.

*Note: A mirepoix is made with medium-sized strips of carrot, celery and onion, with chopped parsley and thyme.

MUSHROOM SOUP

Serves 8

100 g/3¹/₂ oz butter
75 g/2¹/₂ oz flour
1 litre/1³/₄ pints hot milk
1 litre/1³/₄ pints consommé
250 g/9 oz mushrooms, finely chopped
salt
freshly ground black pepper
2 egg yolks
100 ml/3¹/₂ oz single cream

Garnish (optional):
60 g/2 oz mushrooms, sliced and sautéed in
  butter

Left: Crème Agnès Sorel
Below; Crayfish Bisque

Melt the butter in a saucepan, stir in the flour and cook, stirring constantly, for 1-2 minutes until golden. Remove the pan from the heat and gradually stir in the hot milk to make a fairly thick Béchamel sauce. Add the consommé and chopped mushrooms and season with salt and pepper. Return to the heat and simmer for 10 minutes.

Blend the egg yolks with the cream and stir into the soup. Heat through again. If necessary, add a little more hot milk before serving.

Pour the soup into a large tureen, garnish with cooked sliced mushrooms, if liked, and serve immediately.

CREAM OF ASPARAGUS SOUP

Serves 8

200 g/7 oz butter
150 g/5 oz flour
3 litres/5¼ pints chicken stock
500 g/1 lb 2 oz asparagus, chopped
200 g/7 oz asparagus tips
3 egg yolks
200 ml/7 fl oz single cream

Melt half the butter in a saucepan, stir in the flour and cook, stirring constantly, for 1-2 minutes until golden. Remove the pan from the heat and gradually stir in the stock. Return the pan to the heat and bring to the boil, stirring constantly. Remove from the heat and set aside.

Simmer the chopped asparagus in lightly salted water for 8 minutes until tender. Drain, add to the soup base and cook over low heat for 50 minutes.

Cut the asparagus tips into 1 cm/½ inch lengths. Simmer for a few minutes in boiling salted water until just tender. Drain and set aside.

Purée the soup in a blender or food processor and strain into a clean saucepan. Heat almost to boiling point, stirring constantly. Blend the egg yolks with the cream, stir into the soup and heat through, without boiling. Remove from the heat, stir in the remaining butter and transfer to a warm tureen. Garnish with the reserved asparagus tips and serve immediately.

CREAM OF CELERY SOUP

Serves 8

3 celery stalks
60 g/2 oz butter
2 litres/3½ pints water
3 potatoes, peeled and finely sliced
100 ml/3½ fl oz milk
3 egg yolks
100 ml/3½ fl oz single cream
4 slices bread, crusts removed, diced and fried in
   butter
salt

Blanch the celery in boiling water, drain and rinse in cold water. Drain again thoroughly. Chop the celery into chunks.

Melt the butter and lightly fry the celery. Add the water and potatoes and cook over low heat for 1½ hours.

**Top: Oyster Soup à l'Américaine
Bottom Cream of Mussels Soup
Billy By**

Purée the soup in a blender or food processor. Strain into a clean saucepan and add a little milk if the mixture appears too thick. Set over low heat and bring to the boil. Blend the egg yolks with the cream, stir into the soup and heat through, without boiling.

Arrange the hot fried bread cubes in the base of a warm tureen, season the hot soup, pour over the hot, fried bread cubes and serve immediately.

OYSTER SOUP À L'AMERICAINE

Serves 8

4 dozen oysters
2.5 litres/4½ pints water
500 ml/18 fl oz single cream
75 g/2½ oz butter
75 g/2½ crackers or water biscuits, crushed

Discard any oysters that do not close immediately when sharply tapped. Open the shells by inserting the point of a very sharp knife between the two halves, 'feeling' for the weak spot and twisting. You may like to wrap your other hand – the one holding the shell steady – in a towel to prevent injury. Do this over a bowl or plate to ensure that you catch the natural juices.

Measure the oyster juice and add enough water to make up to 2.25 litres/4 pints. Transfer to a saucepan and heat gently for 10 minutes.

Place the oysters (without the shells) in another saucepan. Strain over the hot oyster juice and heat through, without boiling.

Heat the cream and butter together in a small saucepan and blend into the soup with the crushed crackers or water biscuits. Transfer to a warm tureen and serve immediately.

Note: If you are not preparing the oysters immediately after buying them, keep them in their original basket in a cool place, or wrap them, round side downwards, in seaweed or a damp cloth.

CREAM OF MUSSELS SOUP BILLY BY

Serves 4

16 mussels
2 medium-sized onions, peeled and finely
   chopped
1 celery stalk, finely chopped
1 parsley sprig

freshly ground black pepper
100 ml/3½ fl oz dry white wine
250 ml/9 fl oz fish stock or water
250 ml/9 fl oz single cream

Garnish:
1 tbsp chopped parsley

Scrub the mussels under cold running water and discard any that do not shut immediately when sharply tapped.

Place the mussels, onions, celery, parsley sprig and pepper in a saucepan. Add the white wine and fish stock or water and place over high heat. Cover and cook, shaking the pan from time to time, for 5-6 minutes or until the mussels open.

Remove the mussels and discard any that have not opened. Strain the cooking juices through muslin to remove any grains of sand. Remove the mussels from their shells.

Return the cooking liquid to the rinsed-out pan and bring to the boil. Boil until it has reduced by half. Add the cream and bring to the boil, stirring constantly. Add the mussels, season if necessary and serve in soup bowls, garnished with chopped parsley, if liked.

Note: The origins of this soup's unusual name – sometimes spelled 'Bilibi' – are disputed. Some say that it was created by Barthe at the world-famous Maxim's in honour of a customer called Billy, who adored mussels. Others claim that it was created for a farewell dinner given for an American officer called Bill shortly after the Normandy landings in 1944. The name gradually changed from 'Bye bye Bill' to 'Billy By'.

CREAM OF LETTUCE SOUP

Serves 8

4 lettuces
150 g/5 oz butter
2 litres/3½ pints hot milk
salt
freshly ground black pepper

Remove and discard the outer leaves from the lettuces. Blanch the lettuces in boiling salted water for 1 minute. Drain and chop finely.

Melt half the butter and sauté the chopped lettuce for 3-5 minutes. Add the hot milk, season with salt and pepper and simmer for 5 minutes.

Add the remaining butter, transfer to a warm tureen and serve immediately.

For a richer soup, purée the mixture and then blend in 2 egg yolks before serving.

VEGETABLES

AUBERGINES À LA CRÉOLE

Serves 8

16 small aubergines
salt
250 g/9 oz bread, crusts removed
200 ml/7 fl oz milk
200 g/7 oz butter
100 g/3½ oz ham, finely chopped
100 g/3½ oz streaky bacon, finely chopped
½ small onion, peeled and chopped
1 tsp chopped parsley
1 clove garlic, peeled and chopped
100 g/3½ oz breadcrumbs

Cut the aubergines in half, remove the seeds and chop the flesh. Place in a colander and sprinkle with salt. Set aside for 3 hours to dégorge.

Drain the aubergines and rinse under cold running water. Boil in salted water until tender. Drain and purée in a food mill or food processor.

Preheat the oven to 220° C/425° F, gas mark 7.

Soak the bread in the milk. Meanwhile, melt half the butter in a frying-pan and sauté the chopped ham, bacon and onion. Drain the bread and add to the pan with the aubergine purée, chopped parsley and garlic. Cook over high heat for 10 minutes, stirring constantly.

Grease an ovenproof dish with half the remaining butter and pour in the purée. Sprinkle with the breadcrumbs and dot with the remaining butter. Bake in the oven for about 15 minutes.

PRIOR'S SALAD

Serves 4

200 g/7 oz spinach
2 heads chicory
4 tsp tarragon vinegar
¼ tsp paprika
¼ tsp oregano
1 tsp tarragon mustard
2 tsp mayonnaise
60 g/2 oz Parmesan cheese, grated
salt
freshly ground black pepper
100 ml/3½ fl oz olive oil

Wash the spinach, removing any tough stems. Drain and arrange in a salad bowl.

Remove and discard the outer leaves from the chicory and mix the chicory with the spinach.

Combine the vinegar, paprika, oregano, mustard, mayonnaise, Parmesan cheese and salt and pepper to taste. Mix well and blend in the oil. Pour the dressing over the salad. Toss thoroughly so that the salad is well coated and serve.

FENNEL AU GRATIN

Serves 4

6 fennel bulbs
salt
25 g/¾ oz butter
1 tbsp finely chopped ham
450 ml/15 fl oz Béchamel sauce
45 g/1½ oz breadcrumbs
90 g/3 oz Parmesan cheese, grated
freshly ground black pepper

Cook the fennel in boiling salted water for 15-20 minutes until just tender.

Preheat the oven to 180° C/350° F, gas mark 4. Grease an ovenproof dish with the butter.

Drain the fennel, chop roughly and place in the prepared dish. Stir the ham into the Béchamel sauce and pour over the fennel. Combine the breadcrumbs and Parmesan cheese, season and sprinkle over the top. Bake in the oven for 30 minutes.

Serve while hot and bubbling.

AUVERGNE STUFFED CABBAGE

Serves 6

1 large cabbage, trimmed
salt
2 onions, peeled
200 g/7 oz lean bacon, rinds removed and reserved and bacon chopped
200 g/7 oz cooked beef, diced
1 tbsp chopped basil
1 tbsp chopped aromatic herbs (e.g. parsley and thyme)
15 g/½ oz pork fat
freshly ground black pepper

Blanch the cabbage in boiling, salted water for 10 minutes, drain and separate the leaves.

Cook the onions for 15 minutes in boiling, salted water. Drain well and chop.

Preheat the oven to 220° C/425° F, gas mark 7.

Make a stuffing by combining three-quarters of the chopped bacon with the onions, beef, herbs, pork fat, salt and pepper.

Cover the base of an ovenproof dish with the bacon rind and then make alternating layers of cabbage leaves and stuffing mixture, finishing with a layer of cabbage leaves. Top with the remaining bacon. Cover and cook in the oven for about 1½ hours.

Turn the cabbage on to a warm serving dish and garnish as liked. Serve hot.

ASPARAGUS IN MALTESE SAUCE

Serves 8

4 kg/9 lb asparagus
salt

Maltese sauce:
500 ml/18 fl oz Hollandaise sauce
juice of 1 large orange

To prepare the asparagus, wash well and cut off the hard ends. Tie together loosely in a bundle and simmer, upright and covered, in a tall pan of boiling salted water for 15-18 minutes until just tender. Be careful not to overcook the asparagus or it will lose its flavour.

Meanwhile, combine the Hollandaise sauce and the orange juice in a heatproof bowl set over a pan of hot, but not boiling water, or in a bain marie. Heat, stirring constantly, until warmed through. Do not allow the sauce to boil.

Carefully transfer the asparagus to a warm serving dish and remove the string. Pour over the warm Maltese sauce and serve immediately.

Top: Asparagus in Maltese Sauce
Bottom: Auvergne Stuffed Cabbage

ARTICHOKES COUNTRY-STYLE

Serves 6

12 small artichokes
1 lemon, halved
100 ml/3¹/₂ fl oz oil
salt
freshly ground black pepper
1 kg/2¹/₄ lb cooked peas
2 lettuce hearts, coarsely chopped

To prepare the artichokes, pull off the tough outer leaves. Snip off the tops of the leaves with sharp scissors and cut off the stalks about 3 cm/1 inch from the base. Squeeze plenty of lemon juice over the artichokes to prevent discolouration.

Heat the oil in a large flameproof casserole. Add the artichokes, season with salt and pepper, cover and cook for 15 minutes.

Add the cooked peas and chopped lettuce hearts. Cover and cook over low heat for about 1 hour (do not add any water). Serve in the same dish.

MUSHROOM PÂTÉ

Serves 8

8 mushroom caps
100 ml/3¹/₂ fl oz oil
60 g/2 oz butter
1 garlic clove, crushed
2 shallots, peeled and chopped
2 tsp chopped parsley
300 g/10 oz lean bacon, rinds removed and
  diced
300 g/10 oz middle neck of veal, diced
200 ml/7 fl oz single cream
3 egg yolks
100 ml/3¹/₂ fl oz Calvados
700 g/1¹/₂ lb frozen puff pastry, thawed

Blanch the mushrooms in boiling water for 1 minute. Drain and set aside to cool.

Thinly slice the mushrooms. Heat the oil until it is very hot. Dip the mushrooms into the very hot oil to crisp them up. Melt the butter and finish cooking the mushrooms. Remove from the heat and set aside.

Preheat the oven to 180° C/350° F, gas mark 4.

Mix together the shallots, parsley, bacon, veal, cream, egg yolks and Calvados.

Thinly roll out the pastry on a lightly floured surface. Use three-quarters to line the base and sides of a loaf tin. Fill the

Right: Artichokes Country-style
Far right: Mushroom Pâté

dough case with the pâté mixture and top with another layer of pastry. Make a hole in the top for the steam to escape during cooking.

Bake in the oven for 1½ hours. Serve hot, cut into slices and garnished with the mushrooms.

CARROTS LUCULLUS

Serves 8

200 g/7 oz butter
2 kg/4½ lb carrots, trimmed
4 sugar lumps
salt
100 ml/3½ fl oz brandy
2 tsp chopped parsley

Grease a sheet of aluminium foil with 1 tsp of the butter.

Melt the remaining butter in a heavy-based frying-pan, add the carrots, sugar and salt. Cover with the prepared foil and put the pan lid on top. Cook over low heat for 10-15 minutes.

Add the brandy and continue cooking for a further 5-10 minutes. When done, the carrots should be golden and juicy. Serve sprinkled with the chopped parsley.

FENNEL NIÇOISE

Serves 4

4 fennel bulbs, quartered
salt
3 tbsp olive oil
2 garlic cloves, peeled and chopped
2 medium onions, peeled and coarsely chopped
500 g/1 lb 2 oz very ripe tomatoes, skinned and roughly chopped

100 ml/3½ fl oz dry white wine
freshly ground black pepper
¼ tsp dried thyme

Blanch the fennel in boiling, salted water for 10 minutes. Drain.

Heat the oil in a flameproof casserole over low heat. Sauté the garlic and onion for 2 minutes, add the fennel and tomatoes and cook for a further 1 minute.

Add the white wine, season with salt and pepper and stir in the thyme. Cover and cook over a moderate heat for 1 hour.

Transfer the mixture to a warm serving dish and serve immediately.

MUSHROOMS BRILLAT-SAVARIN

Serves 8

60 g/2 oz butter
16 medium mushroom heads
48 canned snails
150 g/5 oz garlic butter*

Preheat the grill to high or preheat the oven to 230° C/450° F, gas mark 8.

Melt the butter in a large frying-pan, add the mushrooms, cover and cook over low heat for 5 minutes.

Add the snails, top with the garlic butter and brown quickly under the grill or in a very hot oven.

*Note: for garlic butter

250 g/9 oz butter
60 g/2 oz shallots, peeled and chopped
2 garlic cloves, peeled and crushed
2 tbsp chopped parsley
salt
freshly ground black pepper
30 ml/1 fl oz Pernod

Left: Carrots Lucullus
Below: Mushrooms
Brillat-Savarin

Mix all the ingredients together to form a smooth paste.

Note: Brillat-Savarin was a gourmet, epicure and world traveller of the late 18th century, who wished to turn gastronomy into a science. He was the author of *Physiologie du goût* (1825) and his name has since been attached to a number of dishes.

ARTICHOKES À LA BÉARNAISE

Serves 8

100 g/3½ oz butter
100 ml/3½ fl oz oil
8 small artichokes
150 g/5 oz ham, finely chopped
2 truffles, finely chopped
500 g/1 lb 2 oz mushrooms, finely chopped
2 sorrel or spinach leaves, finely chopped
200 ml/7 fl oz Béchamel sauce
100 ml/3½ fl oz single cream
100 ml/3½ fl oz white wine
salt
freshly ground black pepper
1 slice bacon, rind removed

Preheat the oven to 180° C/250° F, gas mark 4. Grease a large casserole with the butter and oil.

To prepare the artichokes, pull off the tough outer leaves. Snip off the tops of the leaves with scissors. Cut the stalks and trim the base.

Combine the ham, truffles, mushrooms and sorrel or spinach with the Béchamel sauce, cream and white wine. Season to taste and use to stuff the artichokes.

Arrange the stuffed artichokes in the prepared casserole and top with the slice of bacon. Cover with kitchen foil, put on the lid to prevent the juices evaporating. Bake in the oven for about 1 hour.

Remove the bacon slice and serve hot.

AVOCADO PEARS STUFFED WITH SPINACH

Serves 6

700 g/1¹/₂ lb spinach
3 avocado pears
2 tbsp olive oil
1 onion, peeled and finely chopped
2 hard-boiled eggs, shelled and chopped
salt
200 ml/7 fl oz thick mayonnaise
1 lettuce

Cook the spinach in just the water clinging to its leaves for 8 minutes. Drain well, squeezing out the water, and chop.

Cut the avocado pears in half lengthways. Taking care not to break the skin, remove the stones and the flesh. Chop the flesh and set aside.

Heat the oil and fry the onion until golden. Place in a bowl, add the spinach, avocado flesh and the chopped hard-boiled eggs. Season and mix together well.

Fill the avocado halves with this mixture. Smooth the filling on the top and decorate with mayonnaise. Arrange a bed of lettuce on a serving dish and place the decorated avocado halves on top.

SPRING SALAD

Serves 6

200 g/7 oz roast chicken breast, finely sliced
100 g/3¹/₂ oz radishes, finely sliced
100 g/3¹/₂ oz cooked green beans, finely sliced
100 g/3¹/₂ oz lean ham, finely sliced
75 g/2¹/₂ oz Gruyère cheese, finely sliced
1 green pepper, seeded and finely sliced
2 tomatoes, quartered
1 cucumber, finely sliced
200 ml/7 fl oz olive oil
60 ml/2 fl oz wine vinegar
1 garlic clove, peeled and chopped
salt
freshly ground black pepper

Place the chicken, radishes, beans, ham, cheese, pepper, tomatoes and cucumber in a salad bowl. Beat together the oil, vinegar, garlic, salt and pepper. Pour over the salad, toss thoroughly and serve.

GASCONY MUSHROOMS

Serves 8

16 medium-sized mushrooms
100 ml/3¹/₂ fl oz olive oil
300 g/10¹/₂ oz ham, chopped
1 garlic clove, crushed
1 tbsp chopped parsley
100 ml/3¹/₂ fl oz white wine
salt
freshly ground black pepper

Separate the the mushroom caps from the stalks. Chop the stalks. Heat half the oil and sauté the mushroom caps for 20 minutes.

Put the ham, mushroom stalks, garlic and parsley in a pan and cook over low heat for 2 minutes. Add the white wine, bring to the boil and add the mushroom caps. Season and add a little water if necessary. Cover and cook over a low heat for 35 minutes and serve hot.

Spring Salad

EGG DISHES

EGGS HUGUETTE

Serves 8

1 kg/2¹/₄ lb spinach
150 g/5 oz butter
¹/₄ tsp grated nutmeg
100 g/3¹/₂ oz ham, diced
8 small slices ham
16 eggs
salt

Rinse the spinach well and cook in just the water clinging to the leaves for 8 minutes. Drain, rinse in cold water, drain again and squeeze out any excess water using your hands. Purée the spinach in a blender or food processor.

Melt one-third of the butter in a small saucepan. Add the spinach and the nutmeg and sauté for 15 minutes. Continue to cook, stirring, until the mixture becomes a thick purée.

Remove the pan from the heat, add half the remaining butter and all the diced ham.

Preheat the oven to 180° C/350° F, gas mark 4. Melt the remaining butter and brush 8 small porcelain dishes with it.

Place a slice of ham in each dish and break 2 eggs on top. Sprinkle a little salt over the egg whites and drizzle a little melted butter over the egg yolks. Bake in the oven for 8-10 minutes until the egg whites are just set. Add the cooked spinach to each dish to make a border around the eggs.

BURGUNDY EGGS

Serves 8

16 eggs
1 litre/1³/₄ pints red Burgundy wine
1 onion, peeled and chopped
2 shallots, peeled and chopped
30 g/1 oz mushrooms, peeled, skins reserved
bouquet garni
salt
freshly ground black pepper
60 g/2 oz flour
150 g/5 oz butter
16 slices bread

The eggs may be soft-boiled, hard-boiled or poached.

To make the sauce, place the red wine, onion, shallots, mushroom skins, bouquet garni, salt and pepper in a non-aluminium saucepan. Bring to the boil over a high heat and continue to boil until reduced by about half.

Using a fork, mash together the flour and half the butter to make a *beurre manié*. Add pieces, one by one, to the hot wine mixture, beating constantly. Heat again for a few seconds, remove from the heat and add the remaining butter. Strain the sauce and keep warm.

Serve soft-boiled eggs on bread (rubbed with garlic, spread with butter and then toasted). Serve poached eggs on toast cut into circles. Serve hard-boiled eggs halved. Cover the eggs with the sauce and serve.

Top: Eggs Huguette
Bottom: Burgundy Eggs

OMELETTE CHARLES MONSELET

Serves 8

200 g/7 oz asparagus tips
salt
150 g/5 oz foie-gras, cubed
60 g/2 oz whole mushrooms, fried in butter
2 truffles, finely sliced
16 eggs, beaten
freshly ground black pepper
75 g/2¹/₂ oz butter

Cut the asparagus tips into small pieces. Cook rapidly in boiling, salted water for about 10 minutes until tender. Drain.

Place the foie-gras in a small pan and heat without boiling. Add 4 of the cooked mushrooms, most of the truffle slices and the cooked, drained asparagus.

To make the omelette, beat the eggs together and season with salt and pepper. Melt the butter in a large frying-pan and add the eggs. As soon as it begins to set, add the asparagus filling and fold the omelette over. Turn on to a plate and garnish with the remaining cooked mushrooms and truffle slices.

You may prefer to cook 2 omelettes, each serving 4 people or even 8 separate omelettes, depending on the size of frying-pan or omelette pan.

Note: Charles Monselet was a 19th-century journalist and author of *La Cuisinière poétique* (1859), *Gastronomie* (1874), *Les Lettres gourmandes* (1877) and *Les Mois gastronomiques* (1880). Many dishes have been named after him – particularly ones containing artichokes or truffles – by restaurateurs of the period.

EMERALD OMELETTE

Serves 4

500 g/1 lb 2 oz spinach
3 tbsp olive oil
2 courgettes, chopped
2 leeks, chopped
2 celery stalks, chopped
salt
freshly ground black pepper
6 eggs, beaten
1 tbsp chopped parsley

Prepare and wash the spinach. Cook in just the water clinging to its leaves for 8 minutes. Drain well and chop coarsely.

Heat half the oil in a frying-pan. Sauté the courgettes, leeks and celery for a few minutes. Season with salt and pepper to taste.

Heat the remaining oil in another frying-pan. When it is hot, add the eggs, all the vegetables and parsley and cook until set underneath. Using a plate, turn the omelette over and cook the other side for 2 minutes.

Serve on a round dish, garnished with a few green salad leaves.

EGGS SURPRISE

Serves 8

16 hard-boiled eggs, shelled
60 ml/2 fl oz milk
100 g/3¹/₂ oz fresh breadcrumbs
60 g/2 oz butter
60 g/2 oz Gruyère cheese, grated
salt
freshly ground black pepper
oil for deep-frying

Batter:
3 tbsp flour
salt
1 egg, lightly beaten
450 ml/16 fl oz water

Cut the hard-boiled eggs in half lengthways and remove the yolks. Place the egg yolks in a bowl and mash with the milk, breadcrumbs, butter, grated cheese and a little salt and pepper until the mixture resembles a thick paste. Spoon on to the egg whites.

Make a fairly thick batter. Sift the flour and salt into a bowl and add the egg and half the water. Stir thoroughly to make a smooth paste. Gradually beat in the remaining water. Strain to remove any lumps.

Heat the oil in a deep-fryer to 190° C/375° F or until a cube of stale bread turns golden in 30 seconds. Coat each halved hard-boiled egg with the batter and fry in the hot oil. When the fritters are golden, drain and serve on a dish covered with a folded paper napkin.

SCRAMBLED EGGS À LA D'AUMALE

Serves 8

1 calf's kidney or 2 lamb's kidneys, skinned
salt
freshly ground black pepper
100 g/3¹/₂ oz butter
3 tbsp rich meat stock
60 ml/2 fl oz Madeira
16 eggs, beaten
100 ml/3¹/₂ fl oz fresh tomato sauce
1 tbsp chopped parsley

Clean the kidney(s), remove the core and cut into small cubes. Season with salt and pepper.

Melt 30 g/1 oz of the butter and sauté the kidneys over high heat just long enough to make them firm. Add the rich meat stock, 1 tsp of the remaining butter and the Madeira. Heat gently without bringing to the boil, to prevent toughening the kidneys.

Season the beaten eggs with salt and pepper. Heat half the remaining butter in a saucepan, add the eggs and stir over very low heat. As soon as the eggs begin to solidify, gradually stir in the tomato sauce and the remaining butter in small pieces. The eggs will be ready when they have a thick, smooth consistency.

Turn on to a warmed serving dish and arrange the kidneys in the centre. Garnish with parsley, if liked.

Note: The garnish *à la d'aumale* – used for a variety of dishes – was created by the head chef of Henri d'Orléans, one of the sons of King Louis Philippe.

SCRAMBLED EGGS WITH SMOKED SALMON

Serves 4

8 eggs
salt
freshly ground black pepper
60 g/2 oz butter
2 tbsp double cream
120 g/4 oz smoked salmon, cut into strips
4 slices white bread, crusts removed, lightly fried in butter and cut into triangles

Lightly beat the eggs and season with salt and pepper.

Melt the butter in a heavy-based pan. Pour in the eggs and cook over low heat, stirring constantly with a wooden spoon. As soon as the eggs are just set, remove the pan from the heat and stir in the cream.

Divide the scrambled egg between 4 individual plates and garnish with the strips of smoked salmon and the fried bread triangles. Serve immediately.

Top: Scrambled Eggs à la d'Aumale
Bottom: Omelette Charles Monselet

MUSCOVY EGGS

Serves 4

4 hard-boiled eggs, shelled
8 anchovy fillets
60 g/2 oz caviar or lumpfish roe
8 canned artichoke hearts
100 ml/3½ fl oz aspic jelly, chilled
few pieces of truffle (optional)

Slice the tops and bottoms off the eggs to make them barrel-shaped. Remove the yolk from each egg, through the top end, taking care not to break the white. Wrap an anchovy around each end of the eggs, to form the 'rims' of the barrels. Fill the eggs with the caviar or lumpfish roe, forming a little mound on top of each.

Place each 'barrel' in an artichoke heart. Serve chilled on a bed of chopped aspic, garnished with truffle pieces, if liked.

POACHED EGGS WITH TARRAGON

Serves 4

1 tsp vinegar
8 eggs
4 tarragon sprigs
600 ml/1 pint aspic jelly

To poach the eggs, fill a large frying-pan with water to a depth of 3 cm/1 inch. Bring to the boil, add the vinegar and carefully slide in the eggs, one at a time. Simmer gently for about 4 minutes until the whites are set but the yolks are still soft. Drain and keep in cold water.

Set aside 8 tarragon leaves and chop the remainder. Pour some of the just warm aspic jelly into 8 moulds. Add one tarragon leaf to each mould; it will show through when unmoulded. Allow to set.

Place an egg on top of the set aspic. Combine the chopped tarragon with the remaining aspic jelly and pour over. Chill until set and unmould to serve.

EGG AND CAVIAR FLAN

Serves 4

200 g/7 oz flour
salt
150 g/5 oz butter, diced
6 eggs

2 tbsp milk
freshly ground black pepper
60 g/2 oz caviar or lumpfish roe
juice of 1 lemon

Garnish:
1 hard-boiled egg, shelled and sliced

Sift the flour and some salt on to the work surface. Make a well in the centre and add 75 g/2½ oz of the butter. Work the butter and flour together using the fingers, gradually adding 1-2 tbsp water. Knead until smooth. Set aside in a cool place or in the refrigerator for 1 hour to rest.

Preheat the oven to 180° C/350° F, gas mark 4. Grease a loose-bottomed flan tin with 2 tsp of the remaining butter.

Roll out the pastry on a lightly floured surface and use to line the prepared flan tin. Prick the base with a fork and line with crumpled foil or baking beans. Bake blind in the oven for 30 minutes.

Remove the flan from the oven and set aside, still in the flan tin, on a wire rack to cool. Remove the foil or baking beans.

Beat the eggs with the milk and a little salt and pepper. Pour the mixture into a heatproof bowl set over a pan of hot, but not boiling water, or use a *bain marie*. Stir the mixture until it is beginning to set.

Meanwhile, sprinkle the caviar with the lemon juice. As soon as the eggs are on the point of setting, remove the bowl from the heat and stir in the caviar and the remaining butter.

Remove the pastry case from the flan tin and transfer to a serving dish. Pour the caviar mixture into the pastry case and set aside to cool.

Serve garnished with a few slices of hard-boiled egg.

EGGS MONTROUGE

Serves 4

2 tbsp butter
8 tbsp duxelles (see page 7)
4 eggs
salt
150 ml/5 fl oz double cream

Preheat the oven to 150° C/300° F, gas mark 2. Grease 4 individual egg dishes with the butter.

Pipe a border of duxelles around each dish. Carefully break one egg into the centre of each dish and sprinkle a little salt over the whites. Outline the yolks with a ribbon of cream.

Bake in the oven for 5 minutes or until just cooked. Serve immediately straight from the dishes.

Far Left: Muscovy Eggs
Left: Poached Eggs with Tarragon

FISH AND SEAFOOD

CRAYFISH WITH CREAM

Serves 8

32 crayfish
60 g/2 oz butter
2 shallots, peeled and finely chopped
45 ml/1½ fl oz whisky
60 ml/2 fl oz cherry brandy
90 ml/3 fl oz brandy
500 ml/18 fl oz single cream
salt
freshly ground black pepper

Trim the crayfish by removing the middle fin from the tail and all the intestine attached to it.

Melt the butter and sauté the shallots for 5 minutes, but do not allow them to go golden. Add the crayfish and when they have taken on some colour, add the whisky, cherry brandy and brandy. When the liquid has reduced by half, add the cream and cook for about 10 minutes.

Remove the crayfish and drain them. Reduce the sauce further, if necessary, and season to taste. Serve hot.

MUSSELS WITH SORREL

Serves 6

48 mussels
3 kg/6½ lb sorrel or spinach, cooked and
* drained*
150 g/5 oz butter
60 g/2 oz flour
3 egg yolks
100 ml/3½ fl oz single cream
salt
freshly ground black pepper
250 g/9 oz salt pork or streaky bacon, rinds
* removed and diced*

Scrub the mussels under cold running water and discard any that do not shut immediately when sharply tapped.

Steam the mussels over boiling water until the shells open. Remove from the heat and set aside. Discard any shells that have not opened.

Purée the sorrel or spinach in a blender or food processor. Transfer the purée to a saucepan. Mash half the butter with the flour and stir into the purée over low heat. Stir in the egg yolks and cream and season to taste.

Separate the mussels from their shells. Melt half the remaining butter and sauté the mussels for 2-3 minutes.

Melt the remaining butter and sauté the salt pork or bacon.

Arrange a layer of purée on a serving dish and top with the mussels and salt pork or bacon. Serve immediately.

FILLETS OF SOLE IN PUFF PASTRY

Serves 4

60 g/2 oz butter
1 shallot, peeled and finely chopped
100 g/3½ oz mushrooms, sliced
1 tbsp chopped parsley
8 large sole fillets
salt
freshly ground black pepper
100 ml/3½ fl oz dry white wine

Left: Crayfish with Cream
Right top: Mussels with Sorrel
Right bottom: Fillets of Sole in Puff Pastry

250 g/9 oz frozen puff pastry, thawed
1 egg yolk
200 ml/7 fl oz Hollandaise sauce (optional)

Preheat the oven to 180° C/350° F, gas mark 4. Grease a large ovenproof dish with half the butter and grease a sheet of greaseproof paper with the remainder.

Arrange the chopped shallot, mushrooms and parsley in the dish and place the sole fillets on top. Season with salt and pepper and sprinkle over the wine. Cover the dish with the greaseproof paper and cook in the oven for 10 minutes. When cooked, remove the dish from the

oven and increase the oven temperature to 230° C/450° F, gas mark 8.

Meanwhile, thinly roll out the pastry on a lightly floured surface and cut into 16 rectangles about 12 cm x 7 cm/5 inches x 3 inches.

Place a spoonful of the cooked shallot and mushrooms on 8 of the rectangles and top each one with a sole fillet. Brush the edges of the pastry rectangles with water and place the remaining pastry rectangles on top, pressing down around the edges to form secure parcels. Mix the egg yolk with a little water and brush over the pastry to

glaze. Bake in the oven for 15–20 minutes.

Serve the parcels on their own or with Hollandaise sauce.

HAKE IN TARTARE SAUCE

Serves 8

1.5 kg/3¼ lb hake or cod, in one piece
1 litre/1¾ pints hot vegetable stock
500 ml/18 fl oz Tartare sauce
2 gherkins, sliced
3 hard-boiled eggs, shelled and chopped

Below: Hake in Tartare Sauce
Right: Fish Mousse

Place the fish in a large, shallow flameproof dish and pour over the hot stock. Cover and simmer for 20 minutes.

Remove from the heat and set aside to cool in the cooking liquid.

Drain the fish, divide into portions and place on individual plates. Pour the Tartare sauce around the fish and garnish with the gherkins, and chopped eggs. Serve the remaining sauce separately.

FISH MOUSSE

Serves 8

2 tbsp butter
800 g/1³/4 lb whiting, skinned and boned
150 g/5 oz sliced white bread, crusts removed
200 ml/7 fl oz milk
4 egg whites
500 ml/18 fl oz single cream
salt
freshly ground black pepper
500 ml/18 fl oz creamy tomato sauce

Preheat the oven to 190° C/375° F, gas mark 5. Grease a soufflé dish or 8 individual moulds with the butter.

Cut the fish into small cubes. Soak the bread in the milk, drain and squeeze out most of the liquid. Place the fish, bread and egg whites in a liquidizer and blend to a purée. Slowly add the cream in a thin stream until you have a soft, creamy mixture. Season and turn into the prepared dish or moulds.

Cook in a *bain-marie* or place in a roasting tin half filled with hot water and cook in the oven for about 20 minutes. Serve hot with creamy tomato sauce.

SARDINES STUFFED WITH ALMONDS

Serves 4

1 slice bread, crusts removed
100 ml/3¹/2 fl oz oil
15 g/¹/2 oz currants
12 large, fresh sardines
30 g/1 oz almonds, chopped
salt
freshly ground black pepper
11 bay leaves

Soak the bread in half the oil and soak the currants in boiling water.

Meanwhile, to prepare the sardines, cut off the heads and tails and carefully scrape away the scales. Cut open lengthways along the belly and remove the main bone. Neaten the edges of the sardines with a knife.

Preheat the oven to 200° C/400° F, gas mark 6.

Drain the currants and mix with the bread and chopped almonds. Season with salt and pepper. Place a spoonful of the filling in the opening of each sardine. Arrange the stuffed sardines, side by side, in an ovenproof dish, tightly packed with a bay leaf between each one. Drizzle over the remaining oil and bake in the oven for 15 minutes.

Remove the bay leaves and serve cold.

SOLE À LA MEUNIÈRE

Serves 8

75 g/2¹/₂ oz flour
salt
freshly ground black pepper
8 sole, cleaned
200 g/7 oz butter
juice of 2 lemons
1 tbsp chopped parsley

Season the flour with plenty of salt and pepper and use to coat the sole.

Melt the butter in a large frying-pan and fry the sole for 5-6 minutes, depending on their size.

Place the fried fish on a heated serving dish and pour over the cooking juices. Sprinkle over the lemon juice and chopped parsley and serve immediately.

PRAWNS AU GRATIN

Serves 8

120 g/4 oz butter
500 g/1 lb 2 oz mushrooms, quartered
1 kg/2¹/₄ lb medium-sized prawns, cooked,
   peeled and deveined
3 egg yolks
200 ml/7 fl oz single cream
500 ml/18 fl oz Béchamel sauce
30 g/1 oz crab paste
60 g/2 oz truffles, finely sliced
salt
¹/₄ tsp cayenne pepper
60 g/2 oz Parmesan cheese, grated

Melt the butter in a frying-pan, add the mushrooms, cover and cook for 5 minutes. Stir in the cooked prawns and keep warm.

Preheat the oven to 220° C/425° F, gas mark 7.

Combine the egg yolks with the cream and stir into the Béchamel sauce. Place over low heat and simmer until thickened and reduced slightly. Strain and stir in the crab paste to give a pinkish colour.

Add the sauce to the prawns and mushrooms and stir in the truffle slices.

Season with salt and a little cayenne pepper. Turn the mixture into an ovenproof serving dish or 8 individual shell-shaped serving dishes, sprinkle over the Parmesan cheese and brown in the oven for 5 minutes. Serve immediately.

TROUT IN WHITE WINE

Serves 8

1 onion, peeled and chopped
2 carrots, peeled and chopped
1 celery stalk, chopped
8 trout, cleaned
150 g/5 oz butter
3 tbsp white wine
juice of 2 lemons
salt

Garnish:
8 parsley sprigs
1 lemon, thinly sliced

Place the vegetables in a large frying-pan, add enough water to cover, set over low heat and simmer for 10 minutes until soft. Add the trout, cover and cook for 15 minutes. Drain the trout well and keep hot.

Melt the butter in a saucepan and add the white wine and lemon juice. Season with salt and stir well.

Place the trout on a serving dish, cover with the sauce and garnish with a few slices of lemon and some parsley sprigs, if liked.

SNAILS BOURGUIGNONNE

Serves 8

500 g/1 lb 2 oz butter
30 g/1 oz finely chopped shallots
30 g/1 oz parsley, finely chopped
2 garlic cloves, peeled and finely chopped
¹/₄ tsp ground mixed spice
12 anchovy fillets, chopped
dash of Pernod
salt
freshly ground black pepper
100 canned snails in shells
100 ml/3¹/₂ fl oz dry white wine
100 g/3¹/₂ oz breadcrumbs

To make the flavoured butter, place the butter, shallot, parsley, garlic, mixed spice, anchovy fillets and Pernod in a bowl. Season with salt and pepper and mash thoroughly. Alternatively, work the mixture in a food processor.

Preheat the oven to 220° C/425° F, gas mark 7. To cook the snails, put a knob of

the prepared butter, about the size of a kidney bean, in the base of each snail shell, put a snail into each shell and top with another knob of flavoured butter, pressing the snail well into the shell.

Place the snails in an ovenproof dish and sprinkle over the white wine. Sprinkle the breadcrumbs over the butter at the mouth of each shell. Cook in the oven for 8 minutes.

OYSTERS FRANÇOIS VILLON

Serves 8

4 dozen oysters
75 g/2¹/₂ oz butter
60 g/2 oz flour
500 ml/18 fl oz white wine
500 ml/18 fl oz stock
¹/₄ tsp grated nutmeg
¹/₄ tsp ground ginger
¹/₄ tsp cayenne pepper
100 ml/3¹/₂ fl oz single cream

Discard any oysters that do not shut immediately when sharply tapped. Open the shells by inserting the point of a very sharp knife between the two halves, 'feeling' for the weak spot and twisting. You may like to wrap your other hand – the one holding the shell steady – in a towel to prevent injury. Remove the oysters from their shells and poach in simmering water for 2 minutes. Wash and reserve the shells.

Drain the oysters and cool in cold water. Set aside on paper towels.

Melt the butter in a small pan, stir in the flour and cook, stirring constantly, for 2 minutes. Remove the pan from the heat and gradually stir in the wine, stock, nutmeg, ginger and cayenne pepper. Return the pan to low heat and simmer until golden and creamy. Stir in the cream and heat through gently. Replace the oysters in their shells, pour over the hot sauce and serve immediately.

Top: Snails Bourguignonne
Bottom: Oysters François Villon

RED MULLET À LA BORDELAISE

Serves 8

150 g/5 oz butter
8 x 150 g/5 oz red mullet, cleaned
500 ml/18 fl oz white wine
4 shallots, peeled and finely chopped
500 ml/18 fl oz fresh tomato sauce
2 sprigs tarragon, chopped
salt
freshly ground black pepper

Melt half the butter in a large frying-pan and sauté the fish for 5 minutes. Add the white wine and shallots, bring to the boil, cover and cook for about 12 minutes.

Remove the fish and keep warm. Strain the cooking juices into a saucepan and stir in the tomato sauce. Simmer until reduced and thickened. Remove from the heat and add the remaining butter and the tarragon and season to taste.

Pour the sauce over the mullet and serve.

SEA BASS À LA FINANCIÈRE

Serves 8

1 x 1.5 kg/3¼ lb sea bass, cleaned
2 carrots, peeled and sliced
1 large onion, peeled and sliced
1 bouquet garni
1 litre/1¾ pints water
600 ml/1 pint dry white wine
200 g/7 oz butter
100 g/3½ oz flour
salt
freshly ground black pepper
150 g/5 oz mushrooms, chopped
75 g/2½ oz truffles, finely sliced
200 g/7 oz quenelles (see page 36)

Place the sea bass in a large saucepan together with the carrots, onion, bouquet garni, water and wine. Bring to the boil, cover and simmer for about 30 minutes. Drain and reserve the cooking liquid. Keep hot while you make the sauce.

Melt half the butter in a saucepan. Stir in the flour and cook, stirring constantly, for 2 minutes until golden. Remove the pan from the heat and gradually stir in the reserved cooking liquid. Return the pan to the heat and simmer until thickened. Season to taste.

Meanwhile, heat the remaining butter and sauté the mushrooms for 2 minutes.

Far left: Sea Bass à la Financière
Left: Red Mullet à la Bordelaise

Skin the fish and arrange on a serving dish. Pour over a little of the sauce and garnish with the mushrooms, truffles and quenelles. Serve the remaining sauce separately.

QUENELLES

Serves 6

500 g/1 lb 2 oz white fish fillets, (e.g. sole, hake or whiting), skinned
salt
freshly ground black pepper
5 egg whites
300 ml/10 fl oz double cream

Cut the fish into small cubes, season with salt and pepper and purée in a blender or food processor or work in a food mill. Add the egg whites one by one, blending until the fish has absorbed each egg white before adding the next. Chill in the refrigerator for 1 hour.

Work the mixture with a spatula and gradually stir in the cream. If the cream is too thick, dilute it with a little milk to avoid its curdling and spoiling the quenelles when they are poached.

Meanwhile, bring a small saucepan of water to the boil. Drop teaspoons of the mixture into the water and poach for about 2 minutes until they are soft, yet firm.

LOBSTER À LA PARISIENNE

Serves 8

1 x 1.5 kg/3¼ lb lobster
1.7 litres/3 pints vegetable stock
60 g/2 oz truffles, finely chopped
500 ml/18 fl oz fish gelatine
1 slice bread
1 lettuce, finely shredded
1 litre/1¾ pints mayonnaise
8 canned artichoke hearts
8 hard-boiled eggs, shelled and halved

Lay the lobster on a chopping board to keep the tail flattened. Bring the stock to the boil, plunge in the lobster, cover and simmer for 15-20 minutes. Drain and set aside to cool.

Remove the membrane underneath the tail and remove the meat from the tail, taking care not to break the lobster's shell, which will be used later in the presentation of the dish.

Remove all the meat and the creamy parts from the body of the lobster. Cut the meat into bite-sized pieces and decorate each one with a small piece of truffle and

brush with the fish gelatine. Place the lobster shell on top of the bread slice and press down firmly. Fill the lobster shell and tail with some of the shredded lettuce. Lay the lobster meat pieces on top of the lobster shell, overlapping slightly.

Mix together the remaining lettuce with the lobster shell meat and enough of the mayonnaise and gelatine to bind. Use to stuff the artichoke hearts.

Remove the yolks from the hard-boiled eggs and mix with the remaining truffles and enough gelatine to bind. Fill the egg whites with this mixture. Place the lobster on a serving dish and surround with the garnishes. Serve the remaining mayonnaise separately.

FISH GELATINE

Makes 600 ml/1 pint

2½ tsp gelatine powder
fish trimmings
500 ml/18 fl oz fish stock
4 egg whites, lightly beaten
5 parsley sprigs
5 chervil sprigs
5 tarragon sprigs
30 g/1 oz mushroom peelings
juice of ½ lemon
salt
freshly ground black pepper

Soak the gelatine powder in a little cold water.

Place the fish trimmings and the fish stock in a saucepan and heat through. Add the egg whites, parsley, chervil, tarragon, mushroom peelings, lemon juice and softened gelatine and stir over low heat, without boiling, for 15 minutes.

Strain the stock and add some seasoning if necessary.

SEA BREAM À LA ROCHELAISE

Serves 8

20 oysters
20 small mussels
6 herring roes
250 ml/9 fl oz vegetable stock
250 g/9 oz butter
1 large onion, peeled and chopped
2 x 1 kg/2¼ lb sea bream
salt
freshly ground black pepper
900 ml/1½ pints red wine
1 bouquet garni
60 g/2 oz flour
¼ tsp cayenne pepper

Discard any oysters that do not shut immediately when sharply tapped. Open the oysters by inserting the point of a very sharp knife between the two halves, 'feeling' for the weak spot and twisting. You may like to wrap your other hand – the one holding the shell steady – in a towel to prevent injury. Do this over a bowl or plate to ensure that you catch the natural juices.

Put the oysters and their juices in a pan and poach briefly.

Scrub the mussels under cold running water and discard any that do not shut immediately when sharply tapped. Steam the mussels and discard any that do not open during cooking. Drain and reserve the cooking juices.

Poach the herring roes in the stock for 5 minutes. Drain and cut in half.

Melt 30 g/1 oz of the butter in a frying-pan and sauté the onion for 5-7 minutes until soft but not coloured.

Preheat the oven to 180° C/350° F, gas mark 4.

Cut 3 gashes on each side of the bream to aid the cooking.

Place the sautéed onion in an oval flameproof casserole, arrange the fish on top and season with salt and pepper. Add the wine, reserved mussel cooking juices, 100 g/3½ oz of the remaining butter, diced, and the bouquet garni.

Bring to the boil then cook in the oven for 35 minutes, basting with the juices from time to time.

When cooked, drain the fish and place on a deep serving dish. Garnish with the herring roes, oysters and mussels. Keep hot, but do not return the oven.

Increase the oven temperature to 230° C/450° F, gas mark 8.

Mash together 60 g/2 oz of the remaining butter with the flour to make a *beurre manié*. Strain the fish cooking liquid into a saucepan and beat in the *beurre manié,* one piece at a time. Bring to the boil and cook for a few seconds. Remove from the heat and beat in the remaining butter. Season with the cayenne pepper. Pour the sauce over the fish and the garnish. Return to the oven for a few minutes to glaze the surface of the sauce and serve immediately

LOBSTER À L'AMÉRICAINE

Serves 2

1 x 700 g/ 1½ lb cooked lobster
salt
freshly ground black pepper
210 g/ 7 oz butter
60 ml/2 fl oz olive oil
1 garlic clove, peeled and crushed
½ medium-sized onion, peeled and sliced
3 shallots, peeled and finely chopped
1 carrot, peeled and diced
1 bouquet garni
4 tomatoes, skinned and chopped
250 ml/9 fl oz dry white wine
¼ tsp cayenne pepper
60 ml/2 fl oz brandy
60 ml/2 fl oz sherry
2 tbsp chopped parsley

Split the lobster in half and discard the white gills. Remove and reserve the coral and the liver. Remove all the white flesh, cut into bite-size pieces and season with salt and pepper.

Heat 30 g/1 oz of the butter with the oil in a frying-pan and briefly sauté the lobster pieces. Remove and set aside. Add 60 g/ 2 oz of the butter to the pan and sauté the garlic, onion, shallots and carrot for 8 minutes.

Return the lobster pieces to the pan, add the bouquet garni, tomatoes and white wine. Season lightly with cayenne pepper, cover and cook for 20 minutes.

Meanwhile, mix the lobster coral and liver on a plate with 60 g/2 oz of the butter, using a fork.

Remove the lobster pieces and place on a warm serving dish.

Purée the sauce in a blender, then bring to the boil, add the brandy and sherry and reduce a little. Gradually add the mixture of butter and lobster roe, beating constantly.

Remove from the heat and add the remaining 60 g/2 oz butter to make the mixture creamy. Pour over the lobster and sprinkle over the chopped parsley or garnish as desired.

Lobster à l'Américaine

POULTRY

CHICKEN SOUFFLÉ À LA MODERNE

Serves 6

1 x 1.5 kg/3¹/₄ lb chicken
2.3 litres/4 pints chicken stock
200 g/7 oz butter
75 g/2¹/₂ oz carrots, finely chopped
75 g/2¹/₂ oz leeks, white part only, finely chopped
60 g/2 oz shallots, finely chopped
75 g/2¹/₂ oz celery heart, finely chopped
75 g/2¹/₂ oz mushrooms, finely chopped
1 garlic clove, peeled and crushed
1 tbsp tarragon
¹/₂ tsp chopped thyme
200 g/7 oz minced veal
200 ml/7 fl oz single cream
salt
freshly ground black pepper
100 ml/3¹/₂ fl oz port
75 g/2¹/₂ oz truffles, finely sliced
200 ml/7 fl oz cheese sauce
6 slices bread, crusts removed

Poach the chicken in the chicken stock for 1 hour. Set aside to cool slightly in the liquid.

Melt 60 g/2 oz of the butter in a frying-pan. Add the carrots, leeks, shallots, celery, mushrooms, garlic, tarragon and thyme and a little water. Cover and cook gently for 15 minutes, stirring occasionally.

Preheat the oven to 180° C/350° F, gas mark 4.

Place the veal in a mixing bowl and blend in the cream. Season.

Bring the port to the boil and boil rapidly until reduced by half. Stir the port into the vegetables. Stir in half the veal mixture. Season well.

Place the still warm chicken in a roasting tin. Carefully lift up the chicken breast, making a space between the flesh and the bone, and stuff with the vegetable and veal mixture. Push the chicken back into its original shape. Spread the remaining veal mixture over the chicken and top with a few slices of truffle. Finish cooking the chicken in the oven for 40 minutes, basting occasionally.

Remove the chicken from the oven and increase the oven temperature to 220° C/425° F, gas mark 7.

Carve the chicken breasts into slices and remove the wings and legs. Replace in the roasting tin, pour over the hot cheese sauce and brown in the oven for 20 minutes.

Meanwhile, melt 100 g/3¹/₂ oz of the butter and fry the sliced bread on both sides to make croûtes.

Place the croûtes on a heated serving dish, arrange the chicken pieces on top and pour over the sauce. Melt the remaining butter and drizzle over. Garnish with the remaining truffle slices and extra mushrooms, if liked.

CHICKEN HENRI IV

Serves 8

1 x 2 kg/4¹/₂ lb frozen chicken, with giblets, thawed

Stew:
1 kg/2¹/₄ lb stewing veal, diced
8 small carrots, peeled and roughly chopped
8 small turnips, peeled and roughly chopped
4 leeks, white part only, roughly chopped
1 onion, peeled and roughly chopped
1 marrowbone

Stuffing:
3 chicken livers, chopped
100 g/3¹/₂ oz lean bacon, chopped
100 g/3¹/₂ oz ham, chopped
¹/₄ tsp tarragon
1 garlic clove, peeled and crushed
4 shallots, peeled and chopped
1 tbsp chopped parsley
250 g/9 oz fresh breadcrumbs
2 egg yolks
salt
freshly ground black pepper

Garnish:
1 tsp sea salt
4 gherkins, sliced

First make the stew. Place the veal, carrots, turnips, leeks, onion and marrowbone in a large saucepan or flameproof casserole. Add the giblets from the chicken, pour over just enough water to cover and simmer for 2 hours.

Meanwhile, make the stuffing. Mix together all the ingredients and season with salt and pepper. Use this mixture to stuff the chicken.

Place the chicken on top of the stew, cover and simmer for a further 2 hours or until the chicken is cooked through.

Serve with coarse salt, sliced gherkins and the vegetables from the stew.

Note: You can make a soup with 200 g/7 oz noodles and the cooking stock.

CHICKEN ROQUEFORT

Serves 6

30 g/1 oz sultanas
1 slice bread
100 ml/3¹/₂ fl oz milk
60 g/2 oz Roquefort cheese
60 g/2 oz foie-gras or chicken liver pâté
1 x 1.5-2 kg/3¹/₄-4¹/₂ lb chicken
60 g/2 oz butter
1 tbsp brandy
60 ml/2 fl oz dry white wine
salt
freshly ground black pepper
100 ml/3¹/₂ fl oz single cream

Put the sultanas in a bowl of warm water to soak for 1 hour.

Soak the bread in the milk.

Squeeze out the bread and drain the sultanas. Make a stuffing by combining the cheese with the foie-gras or pâté, bread and half the soaked sultanas. Stuff the chicken with this mixture and sew up the bird with trussing string.

Melt the butter in a large, flameproof casserole. When the butter is very hot, brown the chicken all over. Add the brandy, warm through slightly and ignite. With the flame still alight, add the wine and season with salt and pepper. Cover and cook over low heat for 1¹/₂ hours.

Ten minutes before the end of cooking time, add the cream and the remaining sultanas. Add more seasoning to the sauce if necessary. Serve very hot.

CHICKEN WITH LIME FLOWERS

Serves 6

1 x 1.5 kg/3¹/₄ lb frozen chicken, with giblets, thawed
75 g/2¹/₂ oz butter
salt
freshly ground black pepper

Chicken Roquefort

30 g/1 oz lime flowers★
100 ml/3½ fl oz dry white wine
100 ml/3½ fl oz single cream

Creole rice:
salt
250 g/9 oz rice
60 g/2 oz butter
grated Parmesan cheese (optional)

Joint the chicken into 8 pieces. Reserve the giblets.

Melt the butter in a frying-pan, add the chicken and season with salt and pepper. Cover and cook for 30 minutes.

Meanwhile, prepare the rice. Bring a large pan of salted water to the boil. Add the rice and cook for 12-15 minutes, depending on the type of rice. The rice is ready when it is cooked but still firm to the bite.

Preheat the oven to 140° C/275° F, gas mark 1.

Drain the rice in a colander and rinse with plenty of cold water to prevent it sticking. Drain, place in an ovenproof dish and dot with the butter. Bake in the oven for 15-20 minutes, stirring occasionally with a fork.

Reserve 4 or 5 lime flowers. Uncover the pan of chicken and sprinkle over the remaining lime flowers. Cook for a further 10 minutes. Remove the chicken pieces from the pan and keep warm.

Chop the giblets and add to the pan with the dry white wine. Simmer to reduce for 5 minutes.

Meanwhile, make an infusion with the reserved lime flowers and a little boiling water.

Remove the pan from the heat, add the infusion to the frying-pan and stir in the cream.

Arrange the chicken pieces on a warm serving dish and pour over the sauce. Serve with créole rice. (The rice should be served dry, but not crunchy. If desired, a little grated Parmesan cheese can be added.)

★Note: If lime flowers are unobtainable, use the grated rind and juice of 2 limes.

GUINEA FOWL CHASSEUR

Serves 8

4 thyme sprigs
1 marjoram sprig
1 savory sprig
1 fennel sprig
¼ tsp mixed spice
100 ml/3½ fl oz oil
100 ml/3½ fl oz brandy

3-4 guinea fowl, depending on size
1 kg/2¼ lb wild or cultivated mushrooms
1 garlic clove, peeled and finely chopped
4 shallots, peeled and finely chopped
300 g/10 oz salt pork, diced and cooked
salt
freshly ground black pepper
100 g/3½ oz butter
2 tbsp tomato purée (optional)

Mix together the thyme, marjoram, savory, fennel, spice, half the oil and the brandy. Pour the mixture into the fowl and set aside overnight.

Preheat the oven to 190° C/375° F, gas mark 5.

To prepare the mushrooms, remove the stalks and chop finely. Slice the caps. Mix the stalks and caps with the chopped garlic and shallot to make a stuffing.

Remove the herbs from the birds and discard. Place the birds in a roasting tin with the salt pork and half the remaining oil and roast in the oven for about 1 hour, basting occasionally.

Towards the end of the cooking time, sauté the mushroom stuffing mixture in the remaining oil, season and use to stuff the birds.

To serve, cut each guinea fowl in half and arrange on a warm serving dish with the mushroom stuffing. Deglaze the pan with a little water or vegetable cooking liquid, blend in the butter and tomato purée, if using, and pour over the guinea fowl. Serve very hot.

TARRAGON CHICKEN

Serves 6

120 g/4 oz butter
4 tbsp chopped tarragon
salt
freshly ground black pepper
1 x 2.5 kg/5½ lb chicken

Garnish:
6 tarragon sprigs

Preheat the oven to 190° C/375° F, gas mark 5.

Beat the butter and tarragon together to form a smooth paste. Season with salt and pepper. Stuff half this mixture inside the cavity of the chicken and secure with a skewer or trussing thread. Spread the remaining tarragon butter over the chicken breast.

Place the chicken in a roasting tin and cook in the oven for 30 minutes. Turn the

Guinea Fowl Chasseur

chicken over and roast for a further 30 minutes, basting occasionally with the cooking juices.

Reduce the oven temperature to 180° C/350° F, gas mark 4. Turn the chicken on to its back and baste well with the cooking juices. Roast for a further 30 minutes or until the chicken is cooked through and tender.

Transfer the chicken to a warm serving plate, pour over the cooking juices, garnish with the tarragon sprigs and serve immediately.

TWELVE-AROMA CHICKEN

Serves 4

170 g/6 oz butter
1 x 1 kg/2¼ lb chicken, jointed
1 tbsp port
300 ml/10 fl oz chicken stock

60 g/2 oz carrots, peeled and thinly sliced
60 g/2 oz celery, thinly sliced
60 g/2 oz leeks, thinly sliced
30 g/1 oz chopped shallots
1 garlic clove, chopped
½ tsp dried thyme
½ tsp tarragon
½ dried bay leaf
60 g/2 oz ham, cut in strips
100 ml/3½ fl oz dry white wine
60 g/2 oz mushrooms, sliced
2 tomatoes, skinned and chopped
salt
freshly ground black pepper
1 tbsp chopped parsley

Melt 60 g/2 oz of the butter in a large frying-pan or flameproof casserole and brown the chicken pieces all over. Add the port and chicken stock, cover and simmer for 35 minutes.

Meanwhile, melt 60 g/2 oz butter in another pan and fry the carrot, celery, leeks, shallots, garlic, thyme, tarragon, bay leaf and ham for 2 minutes. Add the white wine and simmer for 15 minutes.

Melt the remaining butter and sauté the mushrooms and tomatoes for 5 minutes.

Stir the vegetable mixture and the mushrooms and tomatoes into the chicken pan, season and heat together for 10 minutes.

Place the chicken pieces on a serving dish, pour over the sauce and sprinkle over the parsley.

STUFFED PIGEONS

Serves 4

1 small bread roll
600 ml/1 pint chicken stock
4 pigeons with giblets
2 tsp chopped parsley
1 garlic clove, peeled and chopped

1 egg yolk
salt
freshly ground black pepper
4 slices streaky bacon
30 g/1 oz butter
1 bay leaf
60 ml/2 fl oz dry white wine

Soak the bread roll in a little stock.

Chop the giblets and place in a bowl with the parsley, garlic and egg yolk. Squeeze the excess liquid from the bread roll and stir in. Season with salt and pepper and mix together well.

Stuff the pigeons with this mixture. Wrap a slice of bacon around each pigeon, pressing down well.

Melt the butter in a large flameproof casserole and add the bay leaf. Brown the stuffed pigeons all over on moderate heat. Season with salt and pepper, add the wine and allow to evaporate slightly.

Reduce the heat, cover and cook the pigeons for about 1¼ hours, turning occasionally and, if necessary, adding a little extra stock to moisten.

Arrange the cooked pigeons on a warm serving dish, remove the bacon and pour over the cooking juices. Serve immediately, with a little Hollandaise sauce if liked.

DUCK STUFFED WITH OYSTERS

Serves 8

6 dozen oysters
2 x 1 kg/2¼ lb ducks with giblets
2 shallots, peeled and chopped
2 eggs
salt
freshly ground black pepper
60 g/2 oz butter
2 carrots, peeled and chopped
2 onions, peeled and chopped
3 tomatoes, skinned and chopped
1 bouquet garni

Preheat the oven to 200° C/400° F, gas mark 6.

Open the oysters (see page 15) and rapidly poach them in their own juices. Set aside to cool and drain.

Finely chop the oysters and the giblets and mix together with the shallots and eggs. Season and use to stuff the ducks.

Melt the butter and sauté the chopped carrots, onions and tomatoes. Place in a roasting tin, add the bouquet garni and arrange the stuffed ducks on top. Roast for 1 hour. Serve hot with the vegetables.

Opposite: Chicken with Lime Flowers (see page 40)
Below left: Stuffed Pigeon
Below right: Twelve-Aroma Chicken

MEAT

SIRLOIN STEAK WITH TARRAGON

Serves 8

200 ml/7 fl oz chicken stock
1 tbsp chopped tarragon
100 ml/3¹/₂ fl oz red wine
200 g/7 oz butter
30 g/1 oz flour
2 x 550-800 g/1¹/₄-1³/₄ lb slices beef sirloin
salt
freshly ground black pepper

Place the stock in a saucepan and boil rapidly to reduce by half.

Preheat the grill to moderate.

Add half the tarragon to the wine and reduce by half. Melt 60 g/2 oz of the butter and stir in the the flour. Remove from the heat and gradually stir in the reduced wine and stock. Simmer over moderate heat to reduce.

Spread the remaining butter on the beef slices and grill them to taste. Season with salt and pepper halfway through the cooking time.

Arrange the beef on a warm serving dish in its own juices. Pour over the sauce and sprinkle over the remaining tarragon.

Below: Sirloin Steak with Tarragon
Right top: Toulouse Cassoulet
Right bottom: Fondue
Bourguignonne (see page 47)

TOULOUSE CASSOULET

Serves 5

500 g/ 1 lb 2 oz dried haricot beans, soaked
overnight and drained
1 thyme sprig
2 bay leaves
500 g/1 lb 2 oz salt pork belly, diced
1 kg/ 2¹/₄ lb boned shoulder of lamb
100 g/3¹/₂ oz butter
1 can tomato purée
2 tbsp Armagnac
salt
freshly ground black pepper
1 Toulouse sausage
60 g/2 oz breadcrumbs

Preheat the oven to 200° C/400° F, gas mark 6.

Place the soaked and drained beans in a large casserole dish. Add the thyme and bay leaves. Arrange the salt pork on top. Add enough cold water to cover, put on the lid and cook in the oven for 15 minutes.

Reduce the oven temperature to 180° C/350° F, gas mark 4 and continue cooking for 2½ hours, adding a little water to moisten, if necessary.

Cut the shoulder of lamb into 10 pieces. Melt half the butter in a frying-pan and sauté the lamb pieces for 30 minutes, then add to the beans and pork. Stir in the tomato purée and the Armagnac, season and return to the oven for 30 minutes.

Meanwhile, cut the sausage into 5 pieces and fry in the remaining butter for 10 minutes.

Remove the casserole from the oven and increase the heat to 220° C/425° F, gas mark 7. Place the sausage pieces on top of the bean mixture and sprinkle over half the breadcrumbs. Return to the oven, uncovered, for 15 minutes.

Remove again, stir the mixture well, sprinkle over the remaining breadcrumbs and cook for a further 15 minutes. Serve very hot.

NORMANDY PORK CHOPS

Serves 8

100 g/3½ oz butter
8 x 150 g/5 oz pork chops
200 g/7 oz cheese, grated
100 ml/3½ fl oz single cream
200 ml/7 fl oz cider vinegar
2 tsp French mustard
salt
freshly ground black pepper

Preheat the oven to 180° C/350° F, gas mark 4.

Melt the butter in a frying-pan and sauté the pork chops on one side only. Place in

a flameproof dish. Mix the cheese and cream together, spread over the chops and cook in the oven for 20 minutes.

Place the chops, upside down, on a serving dish. Deglaze the pan with the vinegar mixed with the mustard. Season, rub through a strainer to obtain a smooth sauce, reheat briefly and pour over the chops. Serve immediately

HAM FLAMBÉ WITH CREAM

Serves 8

100 ml/3½ fl oz wine vinegar
2 shallots, peeled and finely chopped
1 tbsp chopped chervil
1 tbsp chopped tarragon
1 tbsp chopped parsley
4 egg yolks
60 ml/2 fl oz single cream
salt

Below: Ham Flambé with Cream
Left: Normandy Pork Chops

freshly ground black pepper
100 g/3½ oz butter
16 large slices smoked ham
100 ml/3½ fl oz brandy

Put the vinegar, shallots and herbs in a pan and bring to the boil. Boil until reduced to 1 tbsp. Place in a *bain marie* or a heatproof bowl set over a pan of hot, but not boiling water. Stir in the egg yolks and gradually add the cream. Season the sauce and strain.

Melt the butter and sauté the slices of ham. Add the brandy, warm through and ignite. Shake the pan gently until the flames die down.
Serve the ham and the sauce very hot.

FONDUE BOURGUIGNONNE

Serves 6

1 kg/2¼ lb beef sirloin
250 g/9 oz butter
100 ml/3½ fl oz oil
200 ml/7 fl oz fresh tomato sauce
200 ml/7 fl oz sauce griviche
200 ml/7 fl oz mayonnaise

Cut the meat into 1-cm/½-inch cubes.

Heat the butter and oil in the fondue pot and keep hot on the fondue hot plate in the middle of the table.

Each person uses a special long fork with a wooden handle to spear the pieces of meat and dip them into the bowl of hot oil to cook them. Each person should have two side-plates: one to put their raw cubed meat on and another to put their preferred sauce on, to accompany the meat

when cooked. A selection of sauces should be arranged around the fondue set in the centre of the table. The tomato sauce should be served hot and the mayonnaise and the griviche sauce should be served cold. Serve with plenty of fresh bread and a good red wine.

BEEF STROGANOFF

Serves 6

900 g/2 lb sirloin or rump steak
100 g/3½ oz butter
200 g/7 oz mushrooms, sliced
200 g/7 oz gherkins, blanched and sliced

200 ml/7 fl oz soured cream
salt
freshly ground black pepper
juice of 1 lemon
2 tbsp chopped parsley

Trim the steak. Beat flat between 2 sheets of waxed paper and cut into narrow, short strips.

Melt half the butter in a frying-pan and sauté the strips until golden.

Meanwhile, melt the remaining butter and sauté the mushrooms.

Stir the mushrooms and gherkins into the beef. Pour over the soured cream, season with salt and pepper and sprinkle over the lemon juice.

Heat without bringing to the boil, turn into a deep dish, sprinkle with chopped parsley, and serve with green beans.

LAMBS' BRAINS WITH COURGETTES

Serves 4

400 g/14 oz lambs' brains
1 tbsp vinegar
1 small onion, peeled and sliced
1 carrot, peeled and sliced
salt
150 g/5 oz pork loin
90 g/3 oz butter
30 g/1 oz flour
250 ml/9 fl oz warm milk
100 g/3½ oz mushrooms
100 g/3½ oz lean ham, chopped
freshly ground black pepper
2 eggs
170 g/6 oz fresh breadcrumbs
500 g/1 lb 2 oz courgettes, peeled
3 tbsp oil
2 lemons, quartered

Put the brains in a bowl and cover with cold water. Add the vinegar and set aside for 1 hour to soak.

Drain and remove the thin membrane that covers the brains. Place the onion and carrot in a saucepan of lightly salted water. Bring to the boil, add the brains and cook for 10 minutes.

Drain and set aside to cool. Cut the brains into small pieces.

Cut the pork loin into very thin slices. Blanch in boiling water, drain and pat dry.

Melt 30 g/1 oz of the butter, add the flour and stir until well blended. Stir in the warm milk and bring to the boil. Cook, stirring constantly, for 5 minutes.

Remove the pan from the heat and stir in the mushrooms and ham. Spoon 2 tsp of the sauce over each pork slice, top with a piece of brain and a further 2 tsp of sauce. Season and roll up each piece of meat neatly and tie the rolls with string.

Lightly beat the eggs with a little salt. Dip the pork rolls into the beaten eggs and then dip in breadcrumbs, covering the meat well.

Melt the remaining butter in a large frying-pan and fry the rolls until golden.

Meanwhile, cut the courgettes into small sticks and fry in the hot oil.

Place the rolls on a warm serving dish with the fried courgettes in the centre. Serve immediately with lemon quarters.

**Top: Beef Stroganoff
Bottom: Lambs' Brains with Courgettes**

SHOULDER OF LAMB À LA BERRICHONNE

Serves 8

60 g/2 oz bread, crusts removed
60 ml/2 fl oz milk
2 onions, peeled
100 g/3½ oz butter
200 g/7 oz minced pork
2 tsp chopped parsley
1 garlic clove, peeled and crushed
1 egg, beaten
salt
freshly ground black pepper
¼ tsp mixed spice
1.5 kg/3¼ lb shoulder of lamb, boned
8 leeks
3 celery stalks
2 carrots, peeled and quartered
bouquet garni
1 clove
500 g/1 lb 2 oz celeriac, peeled and quartered
4 large potatoes, peeled and quartered

Soak the bread in the milk then squeeze out the excess moisture.

Chop 1 of the onions. Melt 60 g/2 oz of the butter and fry the chopped onion for 5-7 minutes. Set aside to cool.

Combine the bread, fried onion, minced pork, parsley, garlic, beaten egg, salt, pepper and mixed spice in a mixing bowl. Use this mixture to stuff the lamb and tie it securely with string or trussing thread.

Place the lamb in an oval casserole dish, cover with salted water and bring to the boil. Tie the leeks and celery stalks together and add to the casserole with the carrots, bouquet garni and remaining onion, stuck with the clove. Cover and cook over low heat for 1¼ hours.

Add the celeriac, cover and cook for a further 15 minutes.

Add the potatoes and cook for a further 15 minutes.

When all the vegetables are cooked but still whole, drain and reduce to a purée in a blender. Pour the purée into a frying-pan and stir constantly over a high heat until the mixture thickens.

Remove the pan from the heat and add the remaining butter, 1-2 tbsp of the cooking juices from the lamb and seasoning. The vegetable purée should be fairly thick.

To serve, remove the string from the lamb and place it on a warm serving dish. Surround the meat with the vegetable purée. Serve the cooking juices separately.

Shoulder of Lamb à la Berrichonne

NAVARIN PRINTANIER

Serves 6

120 g/4 oz salt pork, diced
700 g/1½ lb boned breast of lamb★, diced
700 g/1½ lb boned shoulder of lamb★, diced
2 tbsp brown sugar
salt
freshly ground black pepper
15 g/½ oz flour
500 g/1 lb 2 oz tomatoes, skinned, seeded and chopped
1.25 litres/2½ pints chicken stock
bouquet garni
60 g/2 oz butter
12 pearl onions
12 new potatoes
6 small turnips
6 small carrots
30 g/1 oz sugar

Fry the salt pork in a heavy-based pan until it has rendered most of its fat. Transfer to a plate and set aside.

Add the lamb to the pan and fry in the pork fat until it is lightly browned all over. Transfer to a plate and set aside.

Drain off about half the pork fat from the pan and return the salt pork and the lamb to the pan. Set over low heat. Sprinkle over the brown sugar and add salt and pepper to taste. Cook, stirring constantly, for 3-4 minutes or until the

sugar has caramelized. Sprinkle over the flour and continue cooking, stirring constantly, for a further 3 minutes.

Remove the pan from the heat and gradually stir in the tomatoes and stock. Return the pan to the heat and bring to the boil, stirring constantly. Add the bouquet garni, reduce the heat, cover and simmer for 45 minutes.

Meanwhile, melt the butter in a large frying-pan and add the pearl onions potatoes, turnips and carrots. Cook for 8-10 minutes until the onions are golden. Add the sugar and cook for a further 2-3 minutes.

Transfer the vegetables to the pan containing the meat. Cook for a further 20-25 minutes or until the meat is tender and the vegetables are cooked through.

Remove the pan from the heat and discard the bouquet garni. Skim any fat from the surface and turn the stew on to a large serving dish or into a tureen.

Serve immediately.

*Note: This spring stew is traditionally made with mutton rather than lamb. If you are able to obtain mutton, trim off any excess fat and increase the cooking time by 15-30 minutes.

BEEF À LA MODE

Serves 4

700 g/1¹/₂ lb rump steak in one piece
1 piece bacon fat
30 g/1 oz butter
¹/₂ calf's foot
250 g/9 oz carrots, peeled and sliced
2 medium-sized onions, peeled
2 cloves
1 bouquet garni
salt
freshly ground black pepper
¹/₂ tsp celery salt
¹/₂ tsp cayenne pepper
¹/₂ tsp paprika
500 ml/18 fl oz dry white wine

Lard the steak with the bacon fat. Melt the butter in a flameproof casserole and sauté the meat until it is light golden. Add the calf's foot, carrots, onions spiked with the cloves, bouquet garni, salt, pepper, celery salt, cayenne pepper and paprika. Stir in the wine and add 60 ml/2 fl oz water. Bring to the boil, cover and simmer over low heat for 3 hours.

Season again, if necessary and if the sauce is too thick, add a little more wine and heat for a few seconds.

Boeuf à la Mode

Place the meat on a warm serving dish, and arrange the carrots, onions and the calf's foot, cut into pieces, around it. Remove and discard the herbs. Skim off the fat from the sauce and pour over the meat. Serve with steamed potatoes.

Opposite top: Breton Pigs' Trotters
Opposite bottom: Calves' Liver with
Apple Sauce
Below: Tournedos Curnonsky

TOURNEDOS CURNONSKY

Serves 8

8 x 120-150 g/4-5 oz tournedos steaks
60 ml/2 fl oz oil
salt
8 mushroom caps
8 medium-ripe small tomatoes
150 g/5 oz butter
2 tbsp chopped parsley
juice of 1/4 lemon
freshly ground black pepper
oil for deep-frying
2 large onions, peeled, sliced and pushed out
   into into rings
100 ml/3¹/₂ fl oz milk
100 g/3¹/₂ oz flour

Preheat the grill to very hot.

Brush the steaks with most of the oil, season with salt and place under the grill. Cook for the desired amount of time, then turn and grill on the other side. Cook each steak according to taste, i.e. rare, medium or well-done.

Brush the mushroom caps and tomatoes with the remaining oil and cook with the steaks.

Place the steaks on a serving dish and top each one with a knob of the butter, some chopped parsley, a squeeze of lemon juice and some freshly ground pepper.

Meanwhile, heat the oil in a deep-fryer to 190° C/375° F or until a cube of stale bread turns golden in 30 seconds.

Dip the onion rings in the milk and then in the flour and deep-fry until golden. Drain on absorbent kitchen paper.

Serve each steak with the onion rings, grilled mushrooms and tomatoes. Accompany with 'pommes dauphinoise', if liked.

BRETON PIGS' TROTTERS

Serves 8

8 semi-salted pigs' trotters
3 litres/5¹/₄ pints white wine
3 litres/5¹/₄ pints brine
1 bouquet garni
3 carrots, peeled
2 onions, peeled
2 cloves
1 garlic clove, peeled
freshly ground black pepper
200 g/7 oz butter, melted
500 g/1 lb 2 oz breadcrumbs
100 ml/3¹/₂ fl oz oil

The fore trotters are more delicate than back trotters and need to be held together with string or a rubber band.

Place the white wine and brine (or one-third vinegar and two-thirds brine) in a large pan. Add the bouquet garni, carrots, onions spiked with the cloves and the garlic. Cover and simmer over low heat for 4-6 hours.

Set aside to cool in the cooking juices.

Light a barbecue or preheat the grill to low.

Drain the trotters and season with pepper. Brush with the melted butter, cover with the breadcrumbs, dip in oil and charcoal-grill over a low fire or grill under low heat, until browned. The cooking time depends on the quality of the meat, but it is better to overcook rather than undercook pigs' trotters. If the cooking juices are adequately seasoned, no accompanying sauce is necessary.

CALVES' LIVER WITH APPLE SAUCE

Serves 4

4 apples, peeled, cored and sliced
1/4 tsp cinnamon
1 clove
30 g/1 oz sugar
60 g/2 oz butter
500 g/1 lb 2 oz calves' liver, sliced
salt
freshly ground pepper to taste

Place the apples in a saucepan with 100 ml/3½ fl oz water, the cinnamon and clove. Cook for 20 minutes over low heat.

Remove from the heat, mash the apples to a purée, add the sugar and cook for a further 5 minutes, stirring constantly.

Melt the butter in a frying-pan and sauté the slices of liver for 2 minutes on each side over high heat. Season with salt and pepper, remove from the heat and serve on a bed of hot apple purée.

TOURNEDOS HENRI IV

Serves 8

8 x 200 g/7 oz tournedos steaks
200 g/7 oz butter, melted
salt
freshly ground black pepper
200 ml/7 fl oz Béarnaise sauce

Light a barbecue★ or preheat the grill to high.

Choose tournedos steaks from the middle of the sirloin. Brush with melted butter then charcoal-grill the steaks, leaving the criss-cross imprint from the grill on them and leaving them a little rare. Season with salt and pepper.

While the steaks are grilling, make a Béarnaise sauce, following the recipe on page 7.

Place the tournedos on a warm serving dish and serve with chipped potatoes and the Sauce Béarnaise.

★Note: Charcoal-grilling gives this dish an especially delicious flavour and makes an attractive criss-cross pattern on the surface of the steak.

The chipped potatoes – potatoes pont-neuf – are traditionally arranged in pairs criss-cross fashion as a garnish. The dish is usually also garnished with watercress.

CALVES' KIDNEYS POMPADOUR

Serves 8

100 g/3¹/₂ oz butter
4 calves' kidneys
6 tomatoes, skinned, seeded and chopped
few drops lemon juice
100 ml/3¹/₂ fl oz brandy
100 ml/3¹/₂ fl oz single cream

Melt half the butter in a frying-pan and sauté the kidneys until rare. Keep hot.

Meanwhile, sauté the tomatoes in the remaining butter. Add a few drops of lemon juice.

Add the brandy to the kidneys' cooking juices. Stir in the tomatoes and cream.

Slice the kidneys into 8 pieces, return to the pan and serve with the sauce straight from the pan.

CALVES' SWEETBREADS FLAMBÉED IN CALVADOS

Serves 8

4 pairs of calves' sweetbreads, soaked for
  2 hours
100 g/3¹/₂ oz butter
8 slices bread, crusts removed
8 Cox's Pippin apples, cored and quartered
100 ml/3¹/₂ fl oz Calvados
500 ml/18 fl oz single cream
salt
freshly ground black pepper

Prepare the sweetbreads: clean, blanch in boiling water, drain and cool. Trim and cut into serving portions.

Melt one-third of the butter in a frying-pan, add the sweetbreads, cover and cook over low heat for 20-30 minutes.

Meanwhile, heat half the remaining butter and fry the bread until golden. Remove and keep warm.

Melt the remaining butter in the pan and fry the apples until just tender.

When the sweetbreads are cooked, add the Calvados. Heat gently and ignite, shaking the pan gently until the flames die down.

Remove the sweetbreads from the pan, stir in the cream and simmer to reduce. Season and serve with the sweetbreads and apple quarters on a warm serving dish.

Left: Tournedos Henri IV
Below: Calves' Sweetbreads Flambéed in Calvados

GAME

ROAST WILD DUCK STEW

Serves 6

1 tbsp butter
3 carrots, peeled and sliced
2 large onions, peeled and sliced
2 wild ducks with giblets
salt
8 slices lean bacon
1 bay leaf

Sauce:
60 g/2 oz butter
2 tbsp flour
100 ml/3¹/₂ fl oz sherry
juice of 1 lemon wedge
salt
freshly ground black pepper
8 green olives, stoned

Preheat the oven to 180° C/350° F, gas mark 4 Lightly grease an ovenproof casserole with the butter.

Place one-third of the carrots, half the onion and the giblets in a saucepan with 750 ml/1¹/₄ pints cold water. Cover and cook for 30 minutes to make a stock.

Meanwhile, rub the ducks with salt. Wrap the bacon around the ducks, making sure to cover the breasts in particular. Add the remaining carrots, onions and the bay leaf to the prepared casserole and place the ducks on top. Cover and cook in the oven for 30 minutes.

Remove and discard the bacon. Cut each duck into 4 pieces and place on an ovenproof dish.

Drain the fat from the carrots and onion. Strain the giblet stock and add to the carrots and onion. Cook over low heat, stirring, until it begins to boil. Simmer to reduce by two-thirds.

Preheat the oven again to 180° C/ 350° F, gas mark 4.

Meanwhile, make the sauce. Melt the butter in a saucepan over low heat. Add the flour and cook for about 10 minutes, stirring occasionally, until golden. Remove the pan from the heat and gradually stir in the reduced duck stock. Return to the heat cooking and bring to the boil, stirring constantly, until it comes to the boil. Add the sherry, lemon juice and salt and pepper to taste.

Strain the sauce, pour over the ducks, cover and cook in the oven for 45 minutes or until the ducks are tender. To test

whether the ducks are cooked, insert a skewer in the flesh. If the juice runs out clear, they are ready. Add the olives and heat again for a few seconds.

Serve accompanied by puréed potatoes and cauliflower.

Note: The commonest and most delicious species of wild duck in France is the mallard, although others, such as the shoveler, are also eaten. If wild duck is not available, farm-bred domestic ducks may be used, but the flavour will not be quite the same.

PHEASANT STEW

Serves 8

100 g/3¹/₂ oz butter
2 pheasants
2 carrots, peeled and finely chopped
1 onion, peeled and finely chopped
2 shallots, peeled and finely chopped
1 bouquet garni
500 ml/18 fl oz white wine
300 ml/10 fl oz reduced chicken stock
250 g/9 oz mushrooms, sliced
150 g/5 oz truffles, sliced
100 ml/3¹/₂ fl oz Madeira wine
100 ml/3¹/₂ fl oz brandy
2 pheasant or chicken livers
60 g/2 oz fatty bacon, finely chopped
8 slices bread, crusts removed and fried in butter
salt
freshly ground black pepper

Melt 30 g/1 oz of the butter and fry the pheasants, turning occasionally, for 20 minutes.

Remove from the pan, take off the skin and cut into joints.

Add the carrots, onions and shallots to the pan, together with 30 g/1 oz of the remaining butter. Sauté until the onions are golden.

Add the bouquet garni and white wine and simmer until reduced by one-third. Stir in the stock, return the pheasant pieces to the pan and add the mushrooms, truffles, Madeira and brandy. Heat gently and ignite, shaking the pan gently until the flames die down. Cover and simmer for about 40 minutes until the pheasant is cooked through.

Meanwhile, melt 30 g/1 oz of the remaining butter and sauté the livers with

the bacon. Work them together in a food mill or food processor to make a purée and spread on the hot fried bread croûtes.

Transfer the cooked pheasant to a warm serving dish. Work the vegetables and cooking liquid in a food processor to form a purée. Briefly heat again, season and stir in the remaining butter. Pour over the pheasant and serve garnished with the prepared croûtes.

RABBIT WITH PEPPERS

Serves 4

100 g/3¹/₂ oz butter
3 tbsp oil
1 wild rabbit, jointed
1 rosemary sprig
1 bay leaf
salt
freshly ground black pepper to taste
200-400 ml/7-14 fl oz stock, as needed
4 red peppers, skinned, seeded and chopped
8 canned anchovy fillets, chopped
2 garlic cloves, crushed
2 tbsp vinegar

Heat half the butter and oil in a heavy frying-pan and sauté the rabbit joints until golden. Add the rosemary and bay leaf, season and cook over a low heat for 1¹/₂ hours, occasionally adding a little stock.

Meanwhile, heat the remaining butter and oil in a frying-pan, add the peppers, anchovies, garlic and vinegar. Season with a little pepper then simmer for 20 minutes over low heat.

When the rabbit is cooked, stir in the red pepper mixture, simmer for 5 minutes and serve hot.

Note: In spite of its reputation for phenomenal fertility, the best edible varieties of French wild rabbit have never fully recovered from the devastation wrought by myxomatosis four decades ago. This epidemic also did irreparable harm to the wild rabbit's reputation as an animal fit for the table. French domestic rabbit is generally a more flavoursome substitute than that available in the U.K., which is often imported deep-frozen.

Top: Pheasant Stew
Bottom: Rabbit with Peppers

HARE À L'ORANGE

Serves 6

1 hare, jointed
2 tsp chopped thyme
1 bay leaf
grated rind of 1 orange
200 ml/7 fl oz red wine
salt
freshly ground black pepper
100 g/3½ oz butter
1 rosemary sprig
2 garlic cloves, crushed

Place the hare pieces in a large, shallow non-metallic dish. Add the thyme, bay leaf and orange rind. Pour over the red wine. Season with salt and pepper. Cover and set aside for 8 hours to marinate, turning the pieces of hare occasionally.

Preheat the oven to 220° C/425° F, gas mark 7.

Drain the hare pieces and arrange in a roasting tin. Reserve the marinade. Add the butter, rosemary and garlic to the roasting tin. Cook in the oven for 15 minutes.

Remove the roasting tin from the oven and lower the temperature to 180° C/ 350° F, gas mark 4.

Pour off the fat and add the reserved marinade. Return to the oven for 2 hours. Place the pieces of cooked hare on a warm serving dish, pour over the cooking juices and serve very hot.

Right: Partridge in Champagne
Below: Hare à l'Orange

PARTRIDGE AU CHAMPAGNE

Serves 4

2 partridges
salt
freshly ground black pepper
150 g/5 oz foie-gras, cubed
60 ml/2 fl oz Cognac
2 slices bacon
100 g/3½ oz butter
100 g/3½ oz mushrooms, sliced
2 slices bread
100 ml/3½ fl oz Champagne
100 ml/3½ fl oz single cream
1 small truffle, thinly sliced

Season the partridges with salt and pepper. Place the cubes of foie-gras in a bowl, cover with the Cognac and set aside to soak for 1 hour.

Drain the foie-gras and use to stuff the

partridges. Wrap a slice of bacon around each partridge and secure.

Melt 60 g/2 oz of the butter in a flameproof casserole and brown the partridges over high heat. Add the mushrooms, cover and cook over medium heat for 1 hour, stirring occasionally.

Meanwhile, melt 60 g/1 oz of the remaining butter in a frying-pan and fry the bread slices on both sides.

When the partridges are cooked, place one on each slice of fried bread and top with the mushrooms. Keep hot.

Add the champagne to the partridge cooking juices, reduce a little, add the cream and remaining butter and simmer to reduce. Pour the hot sauce over the partridges, garnish with the sliced truffle and serve immediately.

QUAILS À LA VIGNERONNE

Serves 8

8 quails
salt
60 g/2 oz butter
100 ml/3½ oz strong veal or chicken stock
2 tbsp grape juice
80 Muscatel grapes, skinned and seeded

Preheat the oven to 220° C/425° F, gas mark 7.

Season the quails with salt. Heat the butter in a flameproof casserole dish and brown the quails all over.

Transfer the casserole to the oven and cook for 12 minutes.

Remove the casserole from the oven, add the veal or chicken stock and bring to the boil. Add the grape juice and the grapes. Heat through for 2 minutes then serve hot.

DESSERTS

CHESTNUT CREAM

Serves 12

150 g/5 oz butter
150 g/5 oz sugar
1 kg/2¼ lb canned unsweetened chestnut
    purée
2 tsp Kirsch or other cherry-flavoured
    liqueur

Cream the butter and sugar together until
light and fluffy. Gradually add the chestnut
purée. Flavour with the Kirsch.

Top: Chestnut Cream
**Bottom: Crêpes Suzette au Grand
Marnier**

CRÊPES

Serves 8

250 g/9 oz flour
¼ tsp salt
4 eggs, beaten
2 tsp olive oil
60 ml/2 fl oz brandy
500 ml/18 fl oz milk

Sift the flour and salt together into a
mixing bowl. Make a well in the centre
and add the beaten eggs, oil and brandy.
Mix thoroughly and add the milk and
enough water to form a smooth batter.
Continue beating until the mixture is
light, airy and lump-free.

Set aside to rest for at least 2 hours
before using.

Make the crêpes by pouring a small
amount of the mixture into a lightly
greased frying-pan over high heat. Tip the
pan to ensure that the batter spreads out
evenly and allow to cook for 1-2 minutes.
Lift the edge of the crêpe with a spatula to
check that the underside is cooked and
golden. If so, flip the crêpe over and cook
the other side for 30-45 seconds.

Cooked crêpes may be kept hot stacked
on a plate, interleaved with greaseproof
paper, set over a pan of hot water.

CRÊPES SUZETTE AU
GRAND MARNIER

Serves 8

6 sugar lumps
1 lemon
2 oranges
100 g/3½ oz butter
24 crêpes
8 tbsp Grand Marnier

Rub the sugar lumps over the lemon and
oranges until soaked with their zest.

Heat the butter in a frying-pan, add the
sugar lumps and heat until bubbling. Dip
each crêpe into the sauce, fold into
quarters and place on a warm serving dish.
Add the Grand Marnier to the pan, heat
gently and ignite. Pour the flaming liquid
over the crêpes and serve immediately.

Note: If Grand Marnier is not available,
other liqueurs may be used.

LEMON CAKE

Serves 8

200 g/7 oz butter
425 g/15 oz flour
¼ tsp salt
2 tsp baking powder
450 g/1 lb sugar
grated rind and juice of 2 lemons
100 ml/3½ fl oz milk
8 egg whites
4 egg yolks
200 ml/7 fl oz double or whipping cream

Garnish:
45 g/1½ oz icing sugar
8-10 cocktail cherries
thinly peeled strips of lemon rind
1 lemon, thinly sliced

Preheat the oven to 180° C/350° F, gas mark 4. Grease a shallow cake tin with 30 g/1 oz of the butter and coat with a little flour.

Sift the flour, salt and baking powder into a mixing bowl and make a well in the centre. Melt the remaining butter. Stir the melted butter, 300 g/10 oz of the sugar and half the lemon rind and juice into the flour mixture. Gradually add the milk and knead the mixture well until smooth.

Beat 6 of the egg whites until fluffy and fold them into the cake mixture.

Pour the mixture into the prepared cake tin. Cook in the oven for 40 minutes. To test whether the cake is cooked, prick with a skewer. The skewer should come out clean if it is cooked through.

Remove the tin from the oven and place on a wire rack to cool completely.

Beat together the egg yolks, the remaining egg whites and the remaining sugar. Add the remaining lemon rind and juice. Beat the cream, mix with the lemon cream. Set aside in the refrigerator for 1 hour to chill.

Turn out the cake on to a serving plate and dust with icing sugar. Pipe a circle of the chilled lemon cream on top and decorate with the cocktail cherries, lemon rind and slices of lemon. Serve with the remaining chilled cream handed separately.

Lemon cake

CHOCOLATE PEARS

Serves 6

60 g/2 oz butter
6 large pears, peeled and halved
100 g/3½ oz sugar
60 ml/2 fl oz white wine
fresh fruit
6 tbsp chopped nuts

Melt the butter in a large heavy-based frying-pan. Add the pears and cook for 5 minutes over a high heat. Add the sugar and the wine and cook for 15 minutes over low heat, until tender.

When the pears are cooked, remove the pan from the heat. Transfer the pears to a dish and set aside to cool.

Meanwhile, place the grated chocolate in a heatproof bowl set over a pan of hot,

but not boiling water or in a *bain marie* and allow to melt, stirring occasionally. Pour the hot chocolate over the pears to coat completely.

Chill in the refrigerator for at least 30 minutes until set. Serve garnished with fresh fruit and chopped nuts.

PINEAPPLE AU CRÈME DE MENTHE

Serves 4

8 pineapple rings, fresh or canned
150 g/5 oz sugar
60 ml/2 fl oz maraschino
3 egg yolks
300 ml/10 fl oz milk
20 g/²/₃ oz flour
2 tbsp crème de menthe

Cover the pineapple rings with half the sugar and the maraschino liqueur. Chill in the refrigerator for 30 minutes, turning occasionally.

Beat the egg yolks with the remaining sugar in a bowl. Add the flour and gradually incorporate the milk and the crème de menthe. Pour this cream into a small saucepan and bring to the boil over low heat, stirring constantly. Cook for 15 minutes, stirring constantly.

Remove the pan from the heat, set aside to cool and then chill in the refrigerator for 30 minutes.

Pour half the creamy mixture on to a serving dish and arrange the pineapple rings on top. Serve the remaining cream in a jug or bowl.

Right: Pineapple au Crème de Menthe
Far right: Chocolate Pears

INDEX